BE YOUR OWN BOSS
VOLUME 1

BE YOUR OWN BOSS

VOLUME 1

18 Reasons Why You Need to Seriously
Consider Becoming Self-Employed
and Minding Your Own Business

TIRI KUIMBAKUL

Copyright © 2019 by Tiri Kuimbakul.

Library of Congress Control Number:	2019918047
ISBN: Hardcover	978-1-7960-0790-9
Softcover	978-1-7960-0789-3
eBook	978-1-7960-0788-6

All rights reserved. No part of this book may be reproduced or transmitted in any form or by any means, electronic or mechanical, including photocopying, recording, or by any information storage and retrieval system, without permission in writing from the copyright owner.

Any people depicted in stock imagery provided by Getty Images are models, and such images are being used for illustrative purposes only.
Certain stock imagery © Getty Images.

Print information available on the last page.

Rev. date: 11/23/2019

To order additional copies of this book, contact:
Xlibris
1-800-455-039
www.Xlibris.com.au
Orders@Xlibris.com.au
804967

ACKNOWLEDGEMENTS

I give God, the source of all wisdom, knowledge and understanding, the praise and glory for empowering me to write this book.

I am thankful to my wife Cathy and our five children for bearing with me as I researched and wrote this book. I know that I have disturbed them many times by getting up at night to jot down ideas as they have come, or to actually write the book, but they have been patient with me.

I am also thankful to Sharon, our eldest daughter, for proofreading the manuscript prior to printing. I am convinced she has done her best. Any factual or grammatical errors are therefore entirely mine.

CONTENTS

Acknowledgements v
Preface ix
Introduction xix

Reason # 1   Jobs are Scarce 1
Reason # 2   Jobs are not Safe and Secure 6
Reason # 3   Earn Several Income Types 15
Reason # 4   Have Multiple Streams of Income 20
Reason # 5   Have Unlimited Earning Potential 28
Reason # 6   Achieve Financial Independence and
             Freedom 39
Reason # 7   Gain Control over Time, One of our
             Most Valuable Resources 47
Reason # 8   Gain Control over Income, Tax and Life 54
Reason # 9   Leverage Other Peoples' Time and
             Skills to get Ahead 61
Reason # 10 Contribute to Job Creation 70
Reason # 11 Develop Better Money Habits 75
Reason # 12 Make Money work for You rather than
             You working for Money 85
Reason # 13 Develop Cost-Consciousness and
             Profit-Mindedness 92
Reason # 14 Realise Your Potential 99
Reason # 15 Develop Your "Survivor's Instinct" 113
Reason # 16 Protect Your Assets 120

Reason # 17 Enjoy Tax Advantages Available to the
             Informal Sector.. 125
Reason # 18 Enjoy Tax Advantages Available to
             Companies 134

Conclusion 143

PREFACE

This book has been written for certain groups of people.

STUDENTS

Firstly, it is for students. Students enroll in school with the hope that they will be able to find jobs with the government or the private sector after they graduate. Parents and relatives spend so much on school fees and associated expenses the day a child starts school until he or she graduates, with the hope that he or she will get a job one day.

The education system is designed to produce employees. Students study various subjects in school with the hope that the knowledge they gain will enable them to find salaried jobs. The system conditions them to expect jobs once they leave school.

What actually happens however is that there are usually not enough jobs for everyone, with the result that only a few succeed in getting jobs. The majority end up with academic qualifications but no jobs. These people are usually labeled as 'failures' or 'drop-outs.'

The education system had prepared them for jobs which are non-existent. They were never taught to create their own jobs, so although they have the potential to become self-employed and do something for themselves, they wander around hopelessly. They go from door to door, and the more they are unsuccessful in securing jobs, the more frustrated they become. Pressure from parents and others who had supported them while in school begin to bear on them as well. They are rejected by those closest to them, so the only place where they find some solace and acceptance is on the streets, where an army of similarly frustrated and hopeless people live.

What is described above is generally the case for the majority of people coming out of the education system. So if you are a student, you would do well to follow as I relate my experiences after I left school. I hope that this book will motivate you to start thinking about becoming self-employed after you leave school.

You may succeed in finding a job. Even then, your long-term security lies in self-employment. But if you find yourself without a job, you will at least know that all hope is not lost. Because you have read this book, you will know that there are options available to you other than a paid job. Not getting a job is not the end of the world; it may in fact be a blessing in disguise.

THE UNEMPLOYED

Secondly, this book is for the unemployed or those currently looking for paid jobs. There are two groups of unemployed people. The first is those who have left school and are looking for their first paid job. This covers both drop-outs and those that have succeeded academically and have graduated with certificates, diplomas and degrees. The second group covers those who have been employed at one stage but have left those jobs either through resignation, termination, retrenchment or for some other reason.

If you are unemployed, I hope that you will find encouragement through this book. I have been unemployed on several occasions. You may identify with my story. I really hope that you will stop thinking about working for someone else, and start thinking about working for yourself. In other words, stop thinking about minding someone else's business and start thinking about minding your own business.

As you will read from my story, I have been unemployed; I have written job application letters; I have knocked on doors looking for employment. But when no door opened for me, I started thinking about creating my own job, and I have succeeded to some extent. At least I have been working for myself over the past two decades. You can do the same. If I and others have done it, you can do it too, but only if you believe you can. I hope to motivate you to believe that you can do something for yourself.

If you are not aware, I have published my first book aimed at providing advice for students leaving secondary school, college and university about various aspects of life after graduation. It is entitled *Life After Graduation*.

If you are a student or a parent, I urge you to obtain a copy of that book, because it discusses many issues concerning work and personal success which students do not learn about in school or at home. Chapter 11 of the book is entitled *"How To Create Your Own Job If Nobody Gives You One."* This book really is an elaboration of the ideas contained in that chapter.

THE EMPLOYED

This book is also for people who are currently employed, that is, working for someone else, be it the government or private businesses. I hope to inspire you to start thinking about how you can become your own boss, instead of working for another person all your life.

You will be ruled and dominated as long as you work for another person. You will be told when to work, when to stop, when to take a break, where to live, and so on. Working for a salary is like slaving to make your employer rich at your own expense.

You will see as you read further that you are in the job only as long as you are useful to your employer. The moment the employer finds somebody better than you, or you reach what the employer judges to be the end of your productive life as far as the organization is concerned, or you reach the official retirement age, you will be shown the door.

I hope that this book will help you prepare for that day. Better still, I hope that you will find encouragement as well as gain the courage to do something for yourself while you are young and have a job. You are in fact better placed to become your own boss eventually, by using your pay wisely. You have an advantage over students and the unemployed because you are receiving an income or seed-money every payday. As I explain in the book, if you treat your job as a source of seed and part of your pay as seed for sowing or investing, it will not be long before you bid your boss goodbye.

Apart from saving and investing part of your pay, you must also learn as much as possible about your job. Take your job as a training ground and transit point towards your ultimate destiny, which is to work for yourself one day. If opportunities arise for further studies, take them. Somebody else (your employer or another sponsor) will pay the cost. To you, it is free training and exposure. Also make as many contacts as you can while you are employed. You never know how useful such contacts can become when you become self-employed.

THE SELF-EMPLOYED

If you are already working for yourself, I would like to assure you that you are on the right track. You have done what the other three groups have yet to do. In that sense you are ahead of them, by miles and years. So keep on going.

You may be facing difficulties. This is normal. Nothing good in life comes free or easy, so keep pressing on. Do not give up. As one of my mentors used to say, "Keep on keeping on."

If you have tried once or several times and failed, remember the following statements successful people have made:

"Winners never quit, and quitters never win."

"Never, never, never give up."

"When the going gets tough, the tough get going."

"Tough times don't last; tough people do."

"Success is 99% failure".

I encourage you to print these statements and pin them on the wall or some prominent place where you can easily see them. Meditate on each of these statements and I can assure you that you will get inspired and motivated to press on.

Thomas Edison, founder of General Electric, is said to have failed 10,000 times in the process of inventing the light bulb. His breakthrough came after 10,000 attempts. Imagine that. You have not tried that many times yet. If you keep trying, your breakthrough will come.

This is what Edison has said from his own experience:

> People who give up too early do not know how close they were to winning when they decided to give up.

What this means is that you may in fact be one failure or setback away from success.

I also encourage you to never for one moment regret that you have launched out to become your own boss. Never for one moment entertain the thought of working for a regular pay. You are free. Going back to work is like heading to jail and slavery. Believe in yourself and keep persisting.

Listen to what John Calvin Coolidge, 30th President of the United States has said about the importance of persistence:

> Nothing can take the place of persistence. Talent will not: Nothing is more common than unsuccessful men with talent. Genius will not: Unrewarded genius is almost a proverb.

Education will not: The world is full of educated derelicts. Persistence and determination are omnipotent. The slogan "press on" has solved and will always solve the problems of the human race.

Sir. Winston Churchill, Prime Minister of the United Kingdom during the Second World War said:

Success is not final and failure is not fatal. It is the courage to continue that matters.

John C. Maxwell has made this statement that has stuck with me for a few years now:

Success is okay so long as it does not get to the head. Failure is fine so long as it does not get to the heart.

If you allow failure to affect your heart, it will cripple you and knock the wind out of you so that you will not have the strength to continue. It won't be long before you give up. On the other hand, if you succeed and it gets to your head, it won't be long before you fall due to pride and arrogance.

Michael J. Lowe has given the following encouragement:

In the pursuit of your victory you may suffer hundreds, possibly thousands, of setbacks, disappointments and frustrations along the way. Remember, however, a champion fight goes 15 rounds. It doesn't matter if you lose a round or two along the way, get up and go again. To rebound from setback and disappointment – that is a sure trait of the victorious in life.

Let these statements encourage you to move on. The people who made these statements spoke from practical experience. As far as I have been able to establish, all these people were successful in what they set out to do or achieve in spite of making many mistakes and facing setbacks.

A friend of mine used to work for himself for some years. But as most of his experience as a business person was one of continual struggle, he decided to look for a job. However, once he got a job, he found that he could not cope with the pressure of getting up early, going to work, clocking in and out, getting instructions from his boss, etc. He could not bear getting permission from somebody else every time he wanted to do something or go somewhere. He found that while he was physically at work, his mind and heart were elsewhere. He did not last at the job.

Today, he is back working for himself with some degree of success. His is the experience of most self-employed people that have tried working for a salary. Once self-employed people have tasted independence and freedom, a paid job rubs against their way of life.

This book is from my heart. I wrote it because I have been challenged by the very high level of unemployment in the country. Many people have complained about the situation and blamed the government for not creating enough jobs to accommodate the thousands of school leavers produced by the education system.

I thought that rather than criticising and joining the whiners, I should open up peoples' minds to the alternatives that are available. I am convinced that the solution to unemployment is not employment but self-employment. The opportunities for self-employment are just too many.

I heard somebody describe Papua New Guinea as 'a businessman's Paradise.' There are too many opportunities around. If you cannot see them, then maybe your mind is closed. Hopefully this book can open your mind to see what the eyes have not been able to see.

Do you know why people of a certain part of the world are flooding our country? They are coming through the door as well as the backdoor and windows, so to speak. They are coming in ship- and plane-loads. If it means for them to pay their way through, they will. If it means for them to pay for their protection from people in high places, they will. The answer is that they can see so many opportunities for making money.

If we local people do not rise up to take advantage of the opportunities, we will continue to be spectators, even though we have more reason to become actively involved in taking up the business opportunities.

I hope that you get challenged and motivated as a result of reading this book. Because it is from my heart, I hope to reach, touch and strengthen your heart. I hope that you can start thinking about being your own boss or minding your own business. I hope that one day you can Be Your Own Boss and have other people call you "Boss," not because you are in charge of a position your employer has created, but because you have built and own the positions those people occupy.

Tiri Kuimbakul
Port Moresby, November 2019

INTRODUCTION

MY STORY

I graduated from the University of Papua New Guinea in 1988 with an Honours Degree in Economics. In 1989 I was fortunate enough to get a job with the Department of Agriculture and Livestock in Port Moresby. I enquired and got the job on the spot because during those days there were many vacancies in Government departments. It is no longer the case today.

THE FIRST SHOCK OF LIFE AFTER SCHOOL

This was when I first encountered my first shock of life after school: *the job did not come with accommodation.* In school accommodation was provided free-of-charge to me. I took it for granted that a house or flat would come with a job. How wrong I was.

I therefore spent the first six months with a school mate. Several of us shared a two-bedroom flat, with three of us 'polishing the floor.' I then moved out to live with an uncle and his family. I stayed with this family for six months, and moved again to stay with another family for the next six months.

Despite the fact that the employer did not provide me with accommodation, I did my best to perform at work. It was not long before the Secretary for Agriculture took notice and nominated me to attend meetings of the then PNG Coffee Industry Board on his behalf.

I had grown up in a coffee-growing family and was familiar with coffee production, but this opportunity enabled me to become involved at a higher level. It was during this brief period that I was introduced to the inner workings of the coffee industry.

A CHANGE OF JOBS

One afternoon I noticed an advertisement in the newspaper concerning a job opportunity with a coffee-exporting company in Goroka. I sat down and wrote a letter expressing interest in the job, sent it off, and forgot about it. A few weeks later I received a call from Coopers and Lybrand, who were the company's recruitment agents, asking me to come for an interview. Following the interview, they called again to say that the company's managers wanted to interview me in person. I attended the interview in Goroka, and was informed two weeks later that they had accepted me for the job.

As soon as I received the news, I submitted a letter of resignation to the Department. The Secretary immediately called me into his office and wanted to know why I wanted to leave. I told him that it was because I did not have accommodation and was tired of moving from place to place.

We spent more than one hour, with him trying his best to convince me to remain because he was impressed with my performance and believed I had a bright future with the Department. He told me that during the past eighteen months that I had been with the Department, I had performed better than many of the long-serving staff. He confessed that in his assessment I was being underpaid, and offered to recommend a pay rise. But I was determined to leave, and told him so.

I left the Department and joined Coffee International Limited in Goroka, then the second largest coffee exporting company in July of 1990.

A FALSE SENSE OF SECURITY

The new employers were good. They paid a better starting salary than the Government. On top of that, they provided a two-bedroom flat and a vehicle for use on a twenty-four hour basis. They even made provision for the school fees for my first child, who was then only six months old. The contract covered personal accident insurance, medical expenses, telephone, electricity, gas and security. They even went as far as providing an allowance for my dog!

It was more than I had expected. It was in fact the dream job for a young man with a young family. The company also had a good training program under which I underwent training in India, Africa and Europe over the next two years.

I was well looked after and was trained for more responsible positions within the company. The Export Manager–an old German coffee trader–even told me that he would groom me to take over from him when he left the company in a few years. Every day he taught me something new about the intricacies of international coffee trading. When I introduced myself to a few expatriates in town, they would say, "*Oh, you are the one old Hugo is grooming.*" I felt so secure and looked forward to a bright future. How wrong I was again, and how false that sense of security was!

The company went into receivership in February 1993 because it had problems meeting its obligations with the bank. With that I lost everything I had enjoyed–literally overnight. Income from the salary ceased. The vehicle, which many people thought belonged to me because of the way I was allowed to use it, and which I also referred to as "my vehicle," had to be returned on the day the bank took over the company's assets. I was given one month to vacate the flat I had been living in and called "my home." I was devastated. I had a very young family, no savings like the majority of working people, and nowhere to go.

Fortunately I had committed my life to God back in 1985, and was attending a church in Goroka. It was the prayers and support of the church people that gave my wife and me the strength to go through this chapter of our lives.

JOB SEARCHING

I spent the next three months looking for another job, but to no avail. I bought newspapers and searched for jobs. I wrote letters to prospective employers in the coffee industry but all the replies I received were negative. World coffee prices were down and the companies were struggling. Some of the companies and organizations I wrote to advised me that there weren't any jobs available at that point in time, but they would keep my letters on file in the event positions became available in future. I realized later that it was a diplomatic way of saying they could not offer me a job, because I never heard from them.

After the fourth month I got a job with the Coffee Industry Corporation as an Economist. The starting salary was not as good as what my previous employers had paid, and many of the other perks were also not provided, but a job was what I needed badly, so I took it gratefully. The only other benefit was a three-bedroom house which had not been occupied for some time. The yard was overgrown with weeds, the power was disconnected, and the walls and floors were dirty, but the state of the house did not concern me as it was better than nothing. So we moved into the house, and I started work life again.

I worked hard at this job, and excelled, such that I was promoted to become one of the Divisional General Managers within six years. This was a very responsible position, and I believe I was the youngest person ever to occupy that position at that time. My experience with the department and the exporting company, and the training I had received while working for the company, enabled me to perform well.

As well as that, I had spent the first two weeks of work in the Corporation's library. I read most of the books and publications and committed the information to memory. I believe these two weeks of reading propelled me to the top within a very short time.

At that time I had developed interest in the international coffee market and how it operates. After reading in the library, I started buying books on the coffee market as well as books related to general export marketing, commodity exchanges, etc.

My job involved several overseas trips in a year. Every time I traveled, I used most of my travel allowances to buy books on coffee marketing and other subjects such as international trade, sales and marketing, public speaking, leadership, finance and stock markets. I still have the stacks of books I have bought with my own money.

Somebody has said, *"Real education starts after the teachers have finished with you."* I am convinced this is true. These books have contributed immensely to me performing well at work, and my being self-employed since 2001.

A CHANGE OF JOBS

In 1999 I resigned to return to the private sector. Many of my friends and associates advised against it, but I left to work for Kongo Coffee Limited as the company's first Export Manager. This position afforded me the opportunity to gain firsthand experience in starting a coffee exporting operation "from scratch."

When I submitted my resignation, the Coffee Industry Corporation refused to accept it. The CEO called me into his office and asked why I was leaving a very secure and high profile job. I told him it was not that I was dissatisfied with anything, but that I wanted to do something different. In his efforts to dissuade me, he offered to raise my salary and other benefits, thinking that I was leaving because of the conditions of employment.

He told me the same thing the Agriculture Secretary had

told me: *that he knew I was underpaid for the amount of work I did, and that he was willing to improve my terms and conditions.* But I had made up my mind.

Fortunately, things did *not* work out as expected, and I lasted only twelve months with Kongo Coffee. In January 2001, I was again without a job. But this time the situation was very desperate because by now I had four children, three of whom were in school. And as is common with the working class, I had not saved much during the years I had been employed. (In fact I made some savings but lost most of it in attempts to start a number of businesses. One small business in particular saw me lose a substantial amount of money, some of it borrowed.)

I had school fees and rent to pay–expenses which were previously met by my employers. And there were many other expenses such as fuel and maintenance for our vehicle besides daily food for a family of six. I could not afford the children's fees for the private school they had been attending, so I pulled them out and enrolled them in a government primary school. Even then I could afford only part of the fees.

JOB SEARCHING AGAIN

This time I looked for jobs for eight months, and came up with nothing. Despite the fact that by now I had twelve years' experience and a very impressive C.V., I just could not get a job. We were behind on our rental payments by many months, and we received several threats of eviction but by the grace of God the landlords accepted our verbal commitments to pay up as soon as we had some money. (We eventually ended up buying the house in 2006!)

It was one of the most difficult and trying times my family and I had been through. To say that it was hard would be to understate the actual situation. Once again we would not have survived without the support of the church. Many times church members would buy us food. One family maintained our vehicle at their cost.

SOME HARD THINKING

It was during this time that I started doing some hard thinking about work, self-employment and financial independence. It began to dawn on me that working for other people was not as safe as I used to think. I realized that it was actually a risky way of living. I also experienced the effect of bad money habits and realized the importance of using money wisely.

It was during this time of contemplation that I registered a business. Even though I had started four different informal businesses in the past and all of them had failed, I did not give up. This time, instead of selling items, I decided to do freelance consulting. I would package and sell information based on my experience as well as from research.

However, even though I had taken a positive step in registering the consulting company, I did not muster the courage to do anything for several months. I still hoped that I would find a job.

A MIND-OPENING AND DESTINY-CHANGING STATEMENT

One day our Pastor called around. In the process of encouraging my wife and I to continue trusting in God to open a door, he said something that really opened my mind and eyes. He pointed to my desktop computer and said, "*Carpenters use hammers and saws; mechanics use spanners and screw drivers; farmers use spades and knives; for you, this computer is a tool which you could use to make a living.*"

This statement triggered something in me. It was as if a light had just gone on inside my head. As soon as he left, I sat at the computer and started typing. Ideas began flying, and in no time I had written an outline of a short course for coffee exporters based on the knowledge I had gathered both from practical experience and from the books I had bought and studied over the years.

It took me about four days to write all the notes and develop a program for a five-day course. I took the outline to the major coffee exporters for their comments, and the response was very positive.

I ran the course two weeks later, and made K12,000 in course fees. This was enough money to pay off all the outstanding school fees and a large part of the rent. I was so amazed. It was unbelievable.

This experience opened my eyes to two things. Firstly, that I did not need a salaried job to live and support my family. I could sell the knowledge I already possessed and make a living with it. This was totally contrary to the one-track mentality I had that having a paid job was the only way

I could sustain my family and I. The experience really opened my mind to possibilities other than living by the pay cheque.

Secondly, and more importantly, I realized that I could make more money if I worked for myself. I used to be paid a salary of K4,000 per month at my last job. The K12,000 I made in those five days was the equivalent of three months' net salary at that job. In other words, in one month I made three times more than I had made for the same period of time working for my employer. And at that point in time the income from the course was tax-free. It dawned on me that I had been under-selling myself to my employers.

When I saw this, I decided there and then that I would never work for a fortnightly pay-cheque again. I did not know how the family and I were going to end up, but what I did know was that being self-employed was going to be our way of life from here on.

A few weeks later I ran another five-day course, and made K7,000, which was enough to bring all rental payments up to date. It took me two weeks to put the course material together and one week to run it. Total time spent: three weeks or one-and-half fortnights; gross income: K7,000 or over K4,666 per fortnight [that is, K7,000 ÷ 1.5 fortnights].

Within the next three months of 2001 I made more than K30,000 from several courses. This was about 65 per cent of the gross salary I would have earned in my last job for the whole year! (I am not trying to boast or impress you by giving you these actual figures. I am merely recounting the thought process I went through which led to me becoming self-employed).

This experience changed the course of my life forever as

far as working for someone else goes. In the first seven years I made more than enough to cover all expenses, with more left over. I was able to invest some of the income in another business which employed one person full-time. I was also able to put up some of the income as equity for a loan to buy and renovate a high covenant house in one of the prime areas of the town, as well as purchase a vehicle with cash for the first time in my working life.

In retrospect, it was good that I could not find a job back in 2001, because had I found a job, I would be living different today. I would in essence be slaving for my employers. I would not have the time to think for myself. My life would be ruled, dominated and controlled. And I doubt that I would have had the experience nor the time to write this book. I would be too busy minding my employer's business.

I know what it means to support a big family without a salaried job. I know what it means to not have food on the table, or not to have money for school fees, rent and other living expenses in a town situation. I know what it means to be threatened with eviction. I know what it means to be abandoned by your closet relatives whom you have supported while you were employed.

IS BEING SELF-EMPLOYED RISKY?

Several working friends I have talked to about self-employment have expressed that they know about the possibilities for bettering their livelihoods if they worked for themselves, but they fear the insecurity that necessarily comes with being self-employed. They have families to feed and children to send to school. They have loans to service. The uncertainties surrounding being self-employed weigh so heavily on their minds that they are unable to start doing something which will eventually see them becoming more and more independent of their employers' pay cheques.

I used to think like that too. My view is completely different. Now, to me, being self-employed is risky in the short-term only, especially if you are already employed. *But in the long-term, hanging onto a job is riskier.*

I am convinced from my own experience that any sense of security you feel in your job is false. Ultimately you will leave the job one day when you retire, if in fact you last that long in the job. My experience as well as research tells me that paid jobs are not as secure as many people are led to believe. *Job security is dead.*

If you are looking for a job, I would like to encourage you to allow and accept the possibility of self-employment into your mindset too. You can look for a job as a short-term measure, but for the long-term, you must still think in terms of becoming self-employed.

EIGHTEEN COMPELLING REASONS TO CONSIDER SELF-EMPLOYMENT

In the following chapters I present eighteen reasons why I believe you need to seriously consider being your own boss. The book is mainly based on personal experience and what I have read and learnt about self-employed people throughout the world. I hope the reasons are compelling enough for you to seriously consider becoming your own boss one day.

I hope to inspire you to be open-minded and to get you to accept self-employment as part of your reality. I have put a lot of thought into this book, because I believe it can change your destiny.

You may think, *"It is easy for you to write about giving your boss the boot and taking his place because you have been through it but I haven't."* My answer to that is, *"If I and millions of others throughout the world have done it, so can you."* It may be a *difficult* prospect for you to contemplate right now, but it is certainly not *impossible*.

If you are a student, I hope to get you to think about working for yourself even while you do your studies. In fact I hope to get you to think and study in anticipation of not getting a job; instead think in terms of creating your own job and becoming an employer rather than an employee. There are not too many jobs available, so don't close your mind to creating your own job.

If you are unemployed, I hope this book will open your mind to the possibility of working for yourself rather than wasting your time writing letters, knocking from door to door, and getting disappointed. Being unemployed can become a blessing in disguise in the sense that you have the opportunity to do something for yourself with your time, skills and knowledge.

If you are employed, I hope the book will make you uncomfortable enough to get you thinking and acting in the direction of self-employment. The message in the book is clear: Having a job is secure in the short-term while working for yourself may seem to be risky. But in the long-term, having a job is riskier, as you can be laid off or terminated anytime.

Your survival in the long run actually lies in being your own boss.

Come with me now for a walk through the eighteen reasons. I believe it is going to be a mind- and eye-opening as well as a destiny-changing journey. It could be the best trip you have ever taken. I can guarantee that you will see things you have never seen before. What you see can change your life and destiny.

REASON # 1

JOBS ARE SCARCE

JOBS ARE SCARCE these days all over the world. In most countries, machines now carry out an increasing volume of work which people used to do. As it costs more to employ people, companies and governments have increasingly sought out ways in which machines such as computers and robots can do what would normally be done by humans. Hundreds of thousands of people have become displaced by machinery, and indications point towards even more mechanization and automation in future.

Other factors which have contributed to the scarcity of paid jobs include corporate mergers and liquidations, downsizing and rightsizing of companies and government organisations with a view to cutting costs and engendering efficiency, and out-sourcing and off-shoring tasks to local and international service providers.

As the world has become more integrated into a "global village," and many trading and employment laws have been relaxed and standardized under the rules of the World Trade Organisation, millions of jobs which could be performed by citizens of a country have become open to competition by non-citizens, and even been taken over by them. This has resulted in many locals missing out on employment opportunities in their own countries.

Out-sourcing and off-shoring have seen thousands of jobs being farmed out to short-term workers and those who come from countries where the cost of labour is perceived to be low.

Nepotism is also rife within both the public and private sectors. It has become so common that today, generally it is *who you know, not what you know.* If you know someone in the system, you have a better chance of getting employed, even if your academic credentials are not that good, or you do not have any experience.

TOO MANY JOB SEEKERS, NOT ENOUGH JOBS

In Papua New Guinea, the number of people coming out of the education system far exceeds the number of new jobs being created by the government and the private sector.

One estimate is that every year about 50,000 people graduate from senior high schools, colleges and universities and enter the job market. In comparison, only 8,000 to 10,000 jobs are available each year. While most of these jobs are new, an increasing number are existing jobs which have been vacated by jobholders due to termination, retrenchment, retirement and disability as well as death through diseases including HIV/AIDS.

So there are over 40,000 people coming out of our educational institutions with certificates, diplomas and degrees but cannot find jobs. Educational institutions are producing workers faster than employers are creating jobs. In other words, there are too many workers chasing too few jobs.

The seriousness of the situation becomes clear when it is considered that in the past, possessing a university degree guaranteed the holder a job. It is no longer the case today. There are so many degree holders in the country who cannot find jobs.

I know of many young people that have graduated from university with a first degree but do not have jobs. Most of these people have been looking for jobs for over one year now. I fear that the longer they do not find jobs, the more their chances for paid employment will decrease, because each year many new graduates come onto the market, and competition for jobs becomes stiffer.

EDUCATED BUT UNEMPLOYED YOUTH: A "TIME BOMB"

Every year the number of drop-outs has been increasing, resulting in the buildup of a large army of educated, unemployed, frustrated and very angry young people in the country. They have been promised the world and given little.

This has led many observers to say that Papua New Guinea is sitting on a "time-bomb." With each passing year the bomb ticks away, and if nothing serious is done to address the high level of unemployment, it will not be long before the bomb explodes. People who can foresee the situation know that the consequences will be dire.

This army is taking control of the streets. You can be somebody in your barbed-wire or corrugated-iron fenced house with security personnel at the gate and be a high-flyer in your profession, but when you hit the streets, you immediately feel insecurity in the air. You cannot walk around without constantly looking at your back. You cannot drive through certain suburbs or settlement areas as you could do in the recent past.

The few employed people are in control of the offices, but the unemployed control the streets. The situation is becoming worse every year. One day the bomb will explode, and people will wonder what went wrong, or why nothing serious was done when the situation was controllable.

THE JOB MARKET IS A BUYERS' MARKET

With too many job-seekers around compared with the number of jobs available, the job market is a buyers' market, meaning that employers have the upper hand in dictating the terms and conditions of employment. In markets where supply exceeds demand, price falls. Likewise, where too many workers are chasing too few jobs, those who are able to get jobs do so at the lowest terms employers can offer.

With the cost of living as high as it is, the majority of working people struggle financially. To some extent they struggle due to financial mismanagement, but much of the struggle is also attributable to salaries which do not keep pace with increasing costs of living.

When employers do raise wages to account for the general rise in the price level, it is usually months and even years late. And the raise usually does not adequately cover the increase in costs of living.

If you are looking for a job, this is the kind of market you are heading for. But is this the right place? You may answer "*Yes.*" You may say, *"Anything is better than nothing."* That may be the correct answer right now in the immediate term. But what about the long-term?

My experience is that employers generally pay their employees just enough to keep them alive and working. Employers are always careful about expenses, and costs related to labour are usually high. It is not only wages but other expenses such as superannuation deductions, housing, leave fares, etc that they take into account. Usually they pay enough to keep their employees happy and returning to work for them.

SELF-EMPLOYMENT: A VIABLE OPTION

I am presenting this information to get you to see that you would be foolish to just limit your thinking to getting a paid job. Unless you know someone in high places, have very good academic credentials or many years of experience, you are most likely going to end up among the majority who do not get jobs.

Even if you have a job now or have been recently laid off for whatever reason, open your mind to the possibility of working for yourself rather than looking for a paid job in a market which is already flooded by job-seekers.

There is really no guarantee that you will get a job, because there just aren't enough jobs to go around. As you read on, I would like to encourage and hopefully convince you to start thinking seriously about self-employment as a viable option.

REASON # 2

JOBS ARE NOT SAFE AND SECURE

IN ADDITION TO jobs being scarce, existing jobs are unsafe. In fact, no job is safe and secure anywhere. I give several reasons for this in Chapter 8 of my book *Life After Graduation*. The chapter is aptly entitled *"Job Security Is Dead*!"

Basically, there have been many changes taking place in the corporate world and in government that have seen the termination, laying off and retrenchment of millions of people all over the world, that a secure job is a thing of the past.

Job security existed during the Industrial Age but in the Information Age, there is no such thing as a safe and secure job. Today's corporate world is very fluid, and so are jobs. Many older companies which have been providing thousands of jobs for decades are finding that they cannot compete with the new Information Age companies which employ small numbers of people but are more efficient and competitive in terms of prices and the quality of goods and services they provide.

EMPLOYEES DO NOT REALLY KNOW WHAT HAPPENS IN AN ORGANISATION

In my experience as related above, the first company I worked with had been in the business for more than thirty years. It was one of the subsidiaries of Rayner Coffee International, a multinational commodity trading company based in the United Kingdom which had been in the business for over seventy years. The mother company had many physical assets like coffee processing mills, offices and houses, not only in Papua New Guinea but also in several countries in Africa and Latin America. Over the years it had successfully withstood several take-over attempts by rival companies as well as long periods of depressed coffee prices. It was the second largest coffee exporting company in Papua New Guinea, earning millions in export revenue.

On the surface the whole group of companies seemed like a formidable organisation. It had withstood the test of time and the turbulences of the coffee market over many decades. This made us employees feel safe and secure. We thought that the company could continue to weather the storms of the international coffee market and that our jobs were secure and our future was safe. It was like living in a lagoon, protected by the company from the vagaries of the marketplace.

But what we the employees did not know was that the local company actually had huge debts owing to the Westpac Bank for which it had mortgaged all its physical assets. As well as that, the mother company in the UK was bankrupt and so was not in a position to support its subsidiaries.

On the surface, it all seemed rosy and we felt secure and

comfortable. We thought we would work in the company for life. I for one thought I had a very bright future ahead of me in this company. The fact that I was being groomed to take over from my expatriate boss when he left provided added comfort.

But underneath, the reality was that the company was on shaky grounds. The company was like a plant that has green leaves and looks healthy on the outside, but is actually being eaten up on the inside by insects. Suddenly the plant turns pale and dies without warning and you ask why or how such a thing could have happened to such a healthy plant.

The top management knew what was coming, but there was no hint given to those of us below them as to the actual situation facing the company.

When the company was finally placed under receivership by the bank and the receivers decided to sell off the assets to recoup what was owed, we were all told to pack up and leave. And the announcement came without prior warning too.

I can vividly recall that morning's meeting. We were all called into the staff room. We thought it was a routine staff meeting. We all made our coffee and mingled around until the boss strolled in. As soon as we looked at his face, we knew that something was wrong. He started by saying some nice things just to "sugar coat the pill," as they say. But when he finally came to the point and broke the bad news, we all got the shock of our lives.

Most of the employees wept openly. It was like a bad dream from which we could not wake up. We all felt like life had gone out of us. We walked out of that office like dead people. All our hopes and dreams disappeared. I believe if a medical check-up was conducted on us that very moment, the doctors would have discovered many funny activities going on in our brains, hearts, and nervous systems.

REAL EXPERIENCES OF FRIENDS I KNOW

I know of several friends who have gone through similar experiences. One got terminated because of some differences with his employer. He was a good worker but just because he could not see eye to eye with the boss on certain matters, he was sacked.

As the saying goes, *the boss is always right*. It is not true that he knows everything and that he is correct all the time, but if you say and do things that put him on the spot, he will fire you in order to save his own face or position. He will make you the scapegoat just to make himself look good, especially if he himself is an employee.

Another friend was laid off because the organisation he was working for went through a restructuring which resulted in his position being made redundant. The bosses decided that the functions he was carrying out were duplications which could be merged into several other positions, and he was assessed to be dispensable, meaning that his leaving would not affect how the organisation operated. In fact with him leaving, the organisation would fare better. He was like excess baggage, a liability.

Yet another was retrenched because the company he was working for faced financial difficulties and had to restructure its operations and cut costs in order to survive. When times had been good, he was considered an asset. Now that times were bad, he had become a liability. I have made this statement elsewhere and I will make it again: *When the going gets tough for the employer, the employee gets going!* My friend had to get going.

A fourth friend was forced to leave because his boss made things difficult for him. The boss had somebody else in line (you guessed it, a wantok!), so he deliberately bullied my friend. The friend was constantly picked on for things that went wrong even though he was not directly responsible. His work was harshly criticised, and the boss indicated to him in many ways both verbally and through his body language that he was not welcome. My friend just could not take it anymore, so he left half-way through his contract. And because he left on his own accord, he had to forego the remaining part of his contractual entitlements.

A fifth friend was forced to retire early because the organisation wanted a younger person. He had many years' experience, but was considered too old, slow and a bit out of date. Younger people could do what he did, and more. So he was shown the door. Fortunately he was a given a "golden handshake" and he is trying to do something for himself.

I have my doubts as to whether he will succeed because all his working life he had depended on the pay cheque. I have observed how he has spent his money when he was working, and I fear that his old money habits will take control of him. In addition to that, he is also physically old. But I may be underestimating him. If he really wants to succeed, he can, despite his age and inexperience as far as business goes.

In all these cases, the employees were not given advance notice of what would happen. All of them were told of their fate unexpectedly. And all of them were shocked when they were finally notified, because they all thought that they would keep their jobs until they retired. Not one of them had ever entertained the thought that he would have to leave the organisation he worked for.

From personal experience and the experiences of these and other friends I know, as well as from reading about what has been happening both in the country and all over the world, I am informing you that there are not many jobs which can be considered safe and secure. *Job security is dead.*

PAID JOBS OFFER A FALSE SENSE OF SECURITY

I see two problems with the sense of security and safety that a job provides. Firstly, it is a false sense of security. If you really dig down to it, you will find how vulnerable you are. When your job is taken away from you, you will discover the real truth.

Secondly, any sense of security you may feel is short-term in nature. You may be secure for a few years but not your whole professional life, and certainly not for life. In the long term, your real security and safety lies in self-employment.

LEARN FROM THE FLYING FOX

Let me give you an illustration using flying foxes. If you go to Madang, you will see hundreds of flying foxes right in the centre of town, hanging up-side-down (to us, but to them, right-side-up!) on branches of trees. If you look closely, you will see that not all of them are clinging to the branches directly. Some of them are in fact clutching onto others who are actually in contact with the branches.

This is a perfect picture of the dependents of someone who has a paid job. The wife, children, parents and relatives look to one person who is the breadwinner. Their wellbeing depends on that one person who has a direct connection to his employer.

When the flying fox which has direct contact with the branches decides to leave his position, he signals with a certain call to everyone holding onto him, so they can fly away before he does. In that way nobody gets hurt.

But imagine what happens when the branch breaks without warning. All of them fall to the ground and get hurt. Some may fly away in midair, but if they have been sleeping, they find themselves on the ground with torn wings. And torn wings are useless to flying foxes.

This is what happens when you cling to a job, and the company goes into receivership or liquidation, which usually comes about to employees without warning. You get hurt, and all your dependents get hurt. All of you fall to the ground as it were, and have to start all over again.

IF YOU WORK FOR YOURSELF, CAN ANYONE SACK YOU?

Let me ask you a question: *If you work for yourself, who can sack you?* The answer is '*Nobody*!' Can you be terminated? Can you get retrenched? Can you be demoted or made redundant? *No!* Why? *Because you are the boss!*

The business you run may fold due to circumstances beyond your control or even as a result of mismanagement on your part, but as long as you work for yourself, you will never be fired. You will never live under the fear of a boss.

I have seen many employees either doing nothing during working hours or doing the wrong thing, and when they see their bosses walking in, they immediately start panicking and doing or pretending to do what they are supposed to do. I have also seen employees going into their boss' offices and apologising to them for being late or explaining why they had been seen at odd places even on weekends.

One lady was playing cards on the office computer and got so carried away that she did not hear the boss entering the room. When he asked her what she was doing, she nearly had a heart attack. Her lips quivered and she began to shiver in her hands and legs. Both guilt and fear could be seen written all over her face.

One day I caught the office driver at an odd place chatting with some people. As soon as he saw my vehicle approaching, he suddenly left his friends on the roadside and drove back to the office in a hurry. His friends must have wondered what had happened for him to just take off like that. When I arrived back at the office, he was waiting to explain what he had been doing at that location. I could see fear in his eyes.

When I was an employee, I tried as much as possible to avoid going to the bank during working hours. During the times that I had to go myself, I used to become restless standing in the queues. I have stood there looking constantly at my watch and wondering what my bosses would be thinking when they called or came into my office and not see me there. I used to feel guilty every time I have been away from office during business hours attending to private matters such as standing in the queue to withdraw money for the family's shopping.

This is the kind of fear all employees live with—the fear of being reprimanded, having their pay docked, being demoted or sacked. If you work for other people, you know what I am talking about.

That is why I am saying that if you want to feel secure and free, create your own job and become the boss. You will be safe from threats of termination and retrenchment, and the heartaches and headaches that go with them. You will also give your dependents a more secure future. You will be a free man or woman.

REASON # 3

EARN SEVERAL INCOME TYPES

FOUR INCOME TYPES

IF YOU HAVE read my second book—*Winning The Game Of Money*—you will know that in Chapter 9 of that book I discuss the four types of income people earn all over the world. They are:

1. *Earned income*, which is income from trading physical labour on a daily basis. The normal words for this type of income are salaries, wages, commissions, bonuses, professional fees, etc.

2. *Passive income*, which is income from a business or real estate. The opposite of passive is active. It is passive, because you do not exert physical strength to earn it. Your employees work for you, or your tenants pay you rent to live in your house or carry out business on your property.

3. *Portfolio income*, which is income earned in the form of dividends which you receive as part-owner of companies. For example, if you become a shareholder of a public company by buying shares on the stock exchange, you receive dividends, which are a certain proportion of the profits the company makes, as decided by the board of directors.

Another way of looking at these three types of income is that passive and portfolio income is income earned by what your money does. Earned income is money you earn from what you do.

4. *Residual income*, which is income in the form of royalties for works of art, copyright over books and patents for inventions. You expend a lot of time and energy writing a book, for instance, for which you get paid over and over every time one of your books is purchased. The labour you put into writing the book or inventing a product or a system has residual value.

Of the four types, earned income attracts the most tax compared to the others. As discussed in Chapter 17, income from salaries and wages, as defined by the Income Tax Act, is highly taxed.

The other important point to note is that earned income flows in only as long as you continue working for your employer. The moment you stop working, the income stops coming. There is no residual value to your time, expertise, talents and strength. The only way to keep money coming in is to go to work every morning.

CONVERTING EARNED INCOME INTO PASSIVE AND PORTFOLIO INCOME

When you become self-employed, in the beginning it may mean you spending a lot of your time and effort building your business. In that sense, what you make is earned income. But after a while you employ people to do what you would do, or purchase a property and rent it out, while you do other things. Then what you earn becomes passive income.

For example, a doctor sets up a private medical clinic, or an accountant sets up an accounting practice to offer services to the public. Or an expert carries out freelance consulting work for clients. These are all examples of working for earned income. If the doctor, the accountant and consultant stop working, there will be no income. So they must keep on turning up for work.

However, after some years let us assume that the doctor, the accountant, or the consultant use the money they make from their businesses to buy properties or shares in other companies. That is the moment they convert earned income into passive and portfolio income. If they receive enough money from their investments, they can afford to stop working and not suffer financially.

REAL-LIFE EXAMPLES

A friend of mine used savings from his salary to purchase a second-hand car from his employer in 1998, which he hired out to clients. The business did so well that he began to add to his fleet. The company has grown quickly and today he has more than twenty new vehicles in his fleet. He also owns a workshop to repair his vehicles and a guest house. He employs more than ten people to run his business, while he only supervises them. This is an example of someone who has successfully converted earned income into passive income.

Another friend purchased a three bedroom house about twenty years ago by putting up his savings as equity and obtaining a bank loan. He lived in his own house, and because he qualified for housing allowance, his employer rented the house from him. He used the rental income to service the mortgage. Some time ago he completed repaying the loan on the house.

Recently he used his house as security to buy a four-unit duplex which he is renting out for a total of K6,000 per month. After meeting mortgage obligations as well as other costs related with owing the property such as insurance and property tax, he has about K600 in net income every month. This is money he does not sweat for. Whether he works or not, the K600 goes into his account every month. The tenants pay for the bank loan, and he makes K7,200 every year.

This is another example of someone who has successfully converted earned income into passive income over a period of over twenty-five years. You can imagine what his passive income will be like after he repays the loan in full and takes ownership of the second property. You can also imagine how easy it will be for him to get a bigger loan for more properties using his two properties as security. He is definitely headed for a future without any need for physical work.

YOU CAN RECEIVE EARNED, PASSIVE AND PORTFOLIO INCOME SIMULTANEOUSLY

The above examples demonstrate that if you work for a salary and manage your money wisely, you can earn the other types of income all at once, especially passive and portfolio income. However, if you are like most working class people, you would be busy working for your boss and paying your taxes, bills and debts that you would not have the money and the time to invest in order to earn passive and portfolio income.

But if you are self-employed, you can easily earn passive and portfolio income. Working for yourself, you would be able to manage your available money more wisely, and thereby have spare cash to invest. The uncertainty surrounding your future without steady income would force you to think more about investing and making your money grow, than focusing on consumption with the mentality that next payday is around the corner.

SELF-EMPLOYMENT OFFERS THE GREATEST POTENTIAL FOR EARNING PASSIVE AND PORTFOLIO INCOME

If you have not figured it out yet, what I am suggesting to you is that you have a better chance of earning money without working hard for it if you are self-employed than if you are somebody's employee. Working for earned income really means selling yourself on a daily basis, while self-employment provides the greatest potential for you to eventually make your money work for you while you take it easy.

REASON # 4

HAVE MULTIPLE STREAMS OF INCOME

WHEN YOU WORK for someone else, your income is from only one source: the fortnightly salary. As stated in Chapter 7, your time is committed to your employer. The employment contract actually binds you to giving full attention to promoting the employer's interests during working hours, which is eight hours from Mondays to Fridays, and sometimes even the weekends.

In this way the cream of your time each working day has been purchased by the employer. Of the twenty-four hours of each day, twelve are in the night and four are early mornings and late afternoons, during which you cannot do much for yourself. If you look into it closely, you will realize that employees commit quality time to serving and advancing the interests of their employers.

EMPLOYEES COMMIT TIME IN ADVANCE; EMPLOYERS PAY FOR TIME IN ARREARS

Note also that even though employees commit their time

to employers "in advance" under the employment contract, employers pay employees "in arrears." This means that employees only get paid after they have worked for their employers.

Employers make certain that they pin down employees' time in advance through contracts, but only pay after they have extracted from employees their time, skills, knowledge, and energy.

As long as an employee is committed to his employer, he cannot work for someone else. If he tries to do it, he will be accused of having a conflict of interests, which is another way of saying that he is trying to serve two masters. So as long as the employee is bound to the employer, he is stuck with only one source of income, and hence livelihood.

For most employees the pay cheque which the employer provides is so important that they cannot imagine living without it. That is why when people are terminated by their employers, they cannot take it.

Most will do everything to cling to their pay cheque. We read of some taking their former employers to court on grounds such as unfair dismissal. We also read of others taking court action to prevent the employers from appointing other people to their old positions. Or when they leave one job on their own accord, they immediately look for another one. There have been many cases of female employees selling their bodies to their bosses just to keep their jobs. A job and the pay cheque are the only ways of living they know.

SELF-EMPLOYMENT GIVES CONTROL OVER TIME

One of the beauties of being self-employed is that you gain control over time, which most people do not realize is one of the most important resources. In fact there are two assets which we all have: *time and our minds*. If you have a sound mind and time, you can succeed anywhere in the world.

Just think about time for a moment. You can conserve all other resources but not time. You can save money in the bank or leave gold in the ground rather than mining it, but you cannot do that with time. Time is unique because it comes and goes. *If you do not use it, you lose it!*

WHEN YOU GAIN CONTROL OVER TIME, YOU CAN DO MANY THINGS

When you take control of time, you can do many things with it. I do not mean you can do several things at the same time, because you cannot. What I do mean is that you can budget your time so that rather than doing one thing all day long–like sitting in an office minding an employer's business–you can do several things for your own benefit.

Let me give you an example. I know of a young man who dropped out of Grade Ten several years ago. He tried to look for a job as a shop keeper but discovered that even such menial jobs are scarce. So he planted vegetables on his land instead. He did not spend any money. He just went to his land, cleared it with his physical strength, and when it was ready, his mother planted sweet potato and other crops. After harvesting and selling what he had planted, he had money in his pocket.

Please note that in his case, he made money without spending any money. I make this point because the world tells people: "*You cannot make money without money.*" Or, "*You must spend money in order to make money.*"

People say that you cannot make money without spending or investing money in the first place. This statement has become so strongly entrenched in people's minds that they really believe that it is impossible to make money without spending money, so they cannot do anything because they do not have money. This is an erroneous belief which is responsible for many people not moving forward to see their dreams and aspirations become a reality.

In this young man's case, he proved the world wrong. *He made money without money.* The statement that you cannot make money without money may apply in developed countries where people do not have land, but not in Papua New Guinea. Here, the young man's experience demonstrates that you can make money without investing money. If you have land, a strong and healthy body, common sense, and the willingness to work, you can make a lot of money just by combining those resources.

Continuing with the young man's story, after he sold vegetables for some time, he built a chicken shed, once again using building materials which he obtained from the bush. When the shed was ready, he used the money which he had earned from the vegetables to buy chicks and stock feed. It cost him around K700 to buy fifty day-old chicks and six bags of stock feed. He used bamboo as watering and feeding troughs, and fire to give warmth and light to the birds. He fed the chickens for eight weeks, after which he sold them for K30 each and made K1,500. When he deducted his expenses of K700, he was left with a profit of K800. This was the equivalent of K200 per fortnight (i.e. K800 ÷ 4 fortnights or 8 weeks).

Let me point out two important lessons here. Firstly, what the young man made in those eight weeks or four fortnights, was more than he would have made had he worked for another person as a shop assistant or even as a security guard. I know for a fact that shop assistants and most security guards receive less than K100 per fortnight. Shop keepers handle a lot of money belonging to their employers, and security guards protect and even defend other people's properties with their lives, but get paid so little for their efforts.

The second lesson, which is the gist of this chapter, is that the young man did two things with his time. He fed the chickens mostly in the mornings and afternoons and checked on them from time to time during the day just to ensure they were fine. But when he was not tending the chickens, he was in his garden working on his vegetables. *He therefore had two income streams.* His life was like a river which is fed by two streams serving as its tributaries.

That is one of the beauties of being self-employed. You can do several things with your time. When you work for other people, you are limited to using your time for their benefit in exchange for a fortnightly salary only.

MANY SETTLEMENT DWELLERS ARE SELF-EMPLOYED AND BETTER OFF

The Papua New Guinea National Research Institute conducted a study of settlements in Port Moresby some years ago. The researchers found that the majority of those who live in settlements do not have any paid jobs. This is not surprising, as we know that settlements are places where the unemployed and underprivileged live.

But contrary to popular belief, what the researchers discovered was firstly that a lot of economic activities take place within the settlements. There are markets, tucker shops, amusement centres such as snooker tables and videos houses, workshops, etc. Secondly, the majority of settlers are self-employed. And even though they are squatting on either state or customary land, an increasing number of them have their own houses, some of which are high-covenant buildings.

This is interesting information for me, because I know that the majority of employed people in Port Moresby and other centres do not have their own houses. They are either living in rented houses, flats and hostels, or bunking up with friends and relatives. They hold high-profile positions and earn a lot of money all right, but they do not have their own houses. They do not have places they can call "home."

In contrast, many settlers do not have jobs and regular income, but they live in their own houses. And many of them have more money than public servants and private sector employees.

Why is this so? I submit to you that one of the main reasons for this seeming contradiction is that the settlers are self-employed, so they have the time to engage in several economic activities and therefore have *multiple streams of income*, whereas those working full time in an office or factory have only one income stream, which is the salary. In addition, the income earned by the settlers is not taxed as they are considered to be operating in the "informal sector," unlike salaries and wages which attract high income tax.

PERSONAL EXPERIENCE

Let me share with you my own experience once again. I used to work as a freelance consultant, which mainly involved conducting research and writing reports for clients. In this capacity I could work for more than one client at any time. I also conducted training workshops and seminars on coffee marketing, stock market investing, academic excellence, personal financial management, etc. Then, I went into book writing and public speaking.

When I did not get consulting work, I would conduct seminars and charge fees. When I was not conducting seminars, I would write. Much of the work I did was complementary as well. For instance, I could easily convert the material in my books into seminars and short courses. The same material could be packaged into several products and sold separately.

So I had several income streams. I liked this, because I could use my time more productively, and more beneficially than if I worked for somebody for a salary. My earning capacity when working for a salary would be limited to the pay cheque, and I would do only what the boss told me to do. As a self-employed person, I worked at my own pace. I allocated my time according to how much I could make from each activity. I had the potential to make more because I had multiple income streams.

I trust that the message is clear. Self-employment offers the possibility of creating and having several streams of income, while having a paid job provides only one source. Which is better for you? I will leave you to answer that question.

REASON # 5

HAVE UNLIMITED EARNING POTENTIAL

WHEN YOU WORK for a fortnightly salary, there is a limit to how much you can earn in a year. Your income will depend on how much you have agreed to with your employer. During the year you might receive traveling and other allowances, and additional income such as commissions and bonuses at the end of the year. Some organizations offer Domestic Market Allowances which are percentages of base salaries. These allowances may be adjusted in line with changes in the job market. But your base salary will remain fixed throughout the year or your contract period, which is usually three years.

Let me give you an example. Say you have an employment contract with your employer, under which you are paid a gross salary of K32,000 per year. That would be K1,231 per fortnight (K32,000 ÷ 26 fortnights).

When you factor in personal income tax using 2019 income tax rates (see Chapter 17 for more on this), your take-home pay would be around K1,031. So the amount of money you take home at the end of every ten working days would be limited.

If you work during the weekends and public holidays, you might receive more for the number of hours worked. Employers usually pay 'time-and-half' or 'double-time' in these instances. But for normal working days, how much you earn will be limited, no matter hard you work each day. If you work less hours, your pay might be docked, in which case you would take less money home. If you work more, you do not get any raise.

REAL INCOME FALLS WITH RISING PRICES

You need to realize that your earning potential is limited when you work for other people. When the cost of living rises, workers do not usually see their income rising proportionately. When prices rise and income remains the same, peoples' *real incomes* decline. In other words, their money's 'buying power' drops such that they either need more money for the same basket of goods and services, or they have to cut back, with a resultant decline in their living standards.

When workers feel the pinch, the only way they can realize increased income is through industrial action. Industrial action usually follows long periods of negotiations where the employers refuse to entertain the workers' demands. Strikes, as they say, are "last resort" actions. Employers are usually reluctant to award salary increases and improvements in terms and conditions of employment, because costs associated with labour are usually high.

When you work for others, what they pay you in a year

remains fixed. The two ways in which you can receive higher income to compensate for increased living costs is through cost of living adjustments or union action. Collaborating with other workers can enable individuals to get better terms. But this is like extortion, or getting something by force, because employers are usually reluctant to pay more. It is usually an act of desperation on the part of employees.

IS THERE A LIMIT TO HOW MUCH YOU CAN EARN WORKING FOR YOURSELF?

Consider this: Is there a limit to how much you can earn by working for yourself being self-employed? If you really think about it, the answer is *"No."*

If you do not succeed in your own business, the risk is that you will lose your initial investment. That is always a possibility. There are no guarantees in life, and there is no guarantee that you will succeed in what you endeavour to do for yourself. The fear of losing hard-earned income in part-time businesses cripples many working people, so they leave their money in the bank and cling to their jobs for their livelihood.

You must be positive about life. Many people tend to quickly think about the negative things that could happen to them, instead of thinking about the good things that can happen when they act in a particular way. Most people live with a very negative mindset, and it shows clearly when they hear about the possibility of becoming self-employed. Their minds quickly ask, *"What if it doesn't work out?"* The fear of leaving a life of regular pay paralyses them into inaction.

Being positive is about risk-taking. It is about stepping out in faith with a positive outlook on life. It is about leaving one's comfort zone and venturing out into deep waters. It is about asking yourself positively, *"What if it does work out?"*

Friend, you need to realize that there is no upper limit to how much you can make when you work for yourself. You may not make money on a daily basis, and your income might be irregular, but when you average out what comes in over time, it would be more than what you would make in a year if you had a job.

Remember me testifying about making K12,000 in five days? If you ask every successful self-employed person, they will tell you the same story. They will tell you that they make more money working for themselves.

WORKING FOR A FORTNIGHTLY SALARY IS A WASTE OF TIME FOR SELF-EMPLOYED PEOPLE

That is why for self-employed people, working for a fortnightly salary is a complete waste of time and life.

Let me give you another personal example. Several years ago I was approached to accept a high-paying and high-profile job. It was tempting. The job came with a high salary, housing and vehicle allowances, school fees, telephone subsidy, medical and life insurance, etc. But I decided not to accept the offer, because I knew that I could make more working for myself than even what that seemingly lucrative offer promised. The opportunity cost of working in that job was too high to my way of thinking.

Let me give you another example. A few years after being

in my own business, I took public transport to the Umi Bridge on the Markham Valley. My vehicle had broken down and I had left it with someone. I was going back with a mechanic to get it fixed.

Sitting next to me was a former employee of the Coffee Industry Corporation. When I asked him where he was going, he replied that he was going to the Umi market to buy peanuts to resell in Goroka. I asked him what life was like now that he did not have a paid job. His reply was, *"Bro, to tell you the truth, I am much better off buying and selling peanuts than I was working for the CIC. I only wish I had left earlier."*

He told me how much money he and his wife were making weekly. He also told me that he could afford to rent a house in a village on the outskirts of Goroka Town. He was able to pay his school fees upfront.

When I heard this story, I thought back to how the betelnut traders in Mount Hagen live. Generally these people earn as well as have more money than the average working person in the country. Most of them live in high-covenant houses which they have built on their own land in their villages, with water supply and electricity connected. And the interesting thing I have noticed is that these people even have domestic servants working for them. They themselves are busy traveling up and down the Okuk Highway buying and selling betel-nuts that they have no time to look after their food gardens and animals such as pigs. They therefore employ other people and pay these people wages to do the gardening, mend their fences, feed their pigs, etc.

I used know of someone who, in his line of work, could make K900 in a day (Note that it is K900 *a day*, not a fortnight!). Multiplying that by 240 working days, he had the potential to earn K216,000 a year. Prior to him becoming self-employed, his gross salary was K8,000 per month or K96,000 a year. That works out to K400 per day. When he was working for himself, he had the potential to earn more than twice what he earned from his former job.

In fact what he could make as a self-employed person was the least, I should say. He could make more if he really pressed himself. For example, he could work for more than one client on any given day, with the result that he doubled or tripled his daily rate. For such a person, it did not make sense to work for someone else for less than he could make working for himself within a shorter period of time. He considered being employed as a waste of time.

I must confess here that I had a hand in this person's decision to get into consulting. A few years earlier I had picked him up from the airport as he was coming back for his usual break from working in a mining company. As we drove around Port Moresby while waiting for his connection flight to Mount Hagen, I advised him to set up his own consulting firm and approach his employer to engage his company as a contractor. I shared with him my story and pointed out to him that with his qualifications and experience, the employer would be willing to enter into such an arrangement. Sure enough, when he returned from break and broached the idea, the company agreed to it. So he ended up with his company being engaged as a contractor, and he made a lot of money.

You may not believe that there are people earning this kind of money. And I am talking about honest money here, not money from some crooked deal. How can some people make K900 (or whatever amount) a day, while you cannot even make so much in a fortnight, even though you are highly educated and have many years of working experience?

You cannot believe it because it lies outside of your imagination and reality. I want to help stretch and expand your mind to accept that such a world does exist. One of the purposes of this book is to help you expand your mind to see possibilities you have never seen before. I have used many real-life examples, including my personal experiences, so that you will know that I am not writing theory here.

The world you know as an employed person is not the only world there is. There is a place where you can earn more than what you are making. And I submit to you that that world is the world of self-employment or business. You can reject the idea that such a world exists, or you can accept it and begin to think about how such a world can become real for you.

EMPLOYEES' INCOMES RISE INCREMENTALLY WHILE EMPLOYERS' INCOMES RISE EXPONENTIALLY

I have held several private sector jobs over the years, and one thing I have noticed is that while the employers' income rises *exponentially*, the employee's income rises *incrementally*. This is another way of saying that there is no upper limit to income for those who work for themselves and employ other people, while their employees' income is fixed and there is a limit to how much more the employees can earn.

Here is an example to help in understanding incremental and exponential growth in income. A friend of mine works as a salesman for a gross salary of K45,000 per year. He has agreed with his employer that if the company's gross sales rise above K600,000, he will be paid a half-percent of the sales plus his base salary. Currently, the company's annual sales are around K400,000. Assume now that sales increase to K650,000. My friend stands to earn an additional K3,250 [0.5% x K650,000]. How much more has the employer made in the year? Of course the answer is K250,000. Who has made more? The employer!

Let us see what this works out in percentage terms. My friend's income has risen from K45,000 to K48,250 – an increase of 7% [(K3,250 ÷ K45,000) x 100]. The employer's income on the other hand has risen by 62.5% [(K250,000 ÷ K400,000) x 100]. How much more has the employer earned compared with the employee? The answer is over seventy six times more!

The employer's income has risen exponentially while my friend has realized only an incremental increase in his income.

If you are a private sector employee and you receive a pay rise, check how much your employer has made. You will realize that what he has made using your talents, skills and expertise has been many times more than what he has paid you.

IS A PAY RISE ACTUALLY WHAT IT LOOKS LIKE?

Employers pay their employees only a small proportion of what the employees make for them. When the employer gives his employees a pay rise, it usually means that the employees made more for him in a year. The pay rise is an incentive the employer provides to maintain the loyalty of his employees. It translates to an incremental change in the pay the employees usually receive. It works out to be a small addition to the employee's normal pay.

What the employees do not realize is that the rise might look enticing in gross form, but when income tax is factored in, the incremental net income actually translates to only a few kina per fortnight. For instance, if your gross pay was K32,000 per year, we have seen that it amounts to a net take-home pay of K1,031 at the end of a fortnight. Now, say the employer gives you a 10% pay rise of K3,200, which takes your gross pay to K35,200 per year. You are elated because your pay has risen by that much.

Has your income really risen by K3,200? The answer is "*No.*" When you take income tax into consideration, what you actually take home every fortnight will have risen by only K81.60, or K2,140 in a year. You have received an incremental income of only K2,140, which works out to a net rise of only 8%, not the 10% you were excited about.

You will not know how much he made, because he will not tell you. And the government will get a pay rise every time you get one too.

Let us also take inflation into account. As we have seen, a rise in the gross salary of K3,200 from K32,000 works out to an increase of 10%. If prices for goods and services have risen by 3% over the same period, your gross *real income* has actually risen by 7%. Not only that. The net or after-tax real income has risen by just 5%.

So although the kina or nominal figure looks exciting, what really matters is what you actually take home, and what you can buy with the money, which in this case would actually be less than it seems to be. Inflation reduces the 'buying power' of your income.

What happens if the inflation rate is more than the pay rise, say 12%? In this case, your real gross income will actually have *fallen* by 2%. When you take account of income tax and inflation, you would actually be worse off in terms of what you can buy, despite that fact that you have received a nominal pay rise of 10%.

So what is the morale of this exercise? It is this: *Do not get overly excited when you get a pay rise or a promotion.* What is important to you is how much you actually take home from a pay rise. You need to look more intently into any rise you get because it may be deceiving. I encourage you to do the above analysis every time you get a raise.

Let me also say that many working people get into financial trouble because they take things at face value. For instance, I have seen so many workers go out and buy things like cars, stereos, TVs, etc just after receiving a promotion or pay rise. And usually they have bought these things with borrowed money. They think that they are better off so they can afford to borrow the money to have these nice things. But if they actually sat down and went through the above exercise to determine what the rise amounts to after tax and taking account of inflation, they would become more prudent managers of their personal finances.

IS THE POSSIBILITY FOR AN EXPONENTIAL INCREASE IN INCOME EXCITING TO YOU?

Let me end this chapter by repeating that when you get into business for yourself, there is no upper limit to how much you can earn. The limit is the sky itself. Your lower limit is that you lose what you invest in whatever venture you start.

What would you prefer to do: Work at a job that provides a regular but fixed income, and hence is more secure, or work for yourself on a venture that is risky but has no upper limit on your earning potential? What is more challenging: Working for an incremental increase or the possibility of an exponential increase in your income?

BE OPEN-MINDED

Each of us is different, so I can understand it if you opt for a job. But please do not block out of your mind the possibility of working for yourself one day. Work for your employer, but also keep the idea of working for yourself at the back of your mind.

I hope that what I have shared with you in this chapter and the rest of the book will help you live with an open mind, not a one-track mind that thinks only about finding and keeping a paid job.

A one-track mind will blind you to other possibilities of living, while being open-minded can enable you to see that there are ways of living other than looking up to the employer for your livelihood.

REASON # 6

ACHIEVE FINANCIAL INDEPENDENCE AND FREEDOM

THE SIXTH REASON you need to think about business is that a job does not provide much opportunity for you to become financially independent and free.

WHAT FINANCIAL INDEPENDENCE IS

Financial independence means that you do not depend on someone else for your livelihood. In other words, you do not need a job and the pay cheque that comes with it in order to survive. You have your own source of income and livelihood. You are financially and economically independent and self-reliant.

Many commentators say that even though Papua New Guinea became politically independent in September 1975, economically it is still dependent on aid from other countries, particularly Australia. They say Papua New Guinea is politically independent but economically dependent. This is because a large proportion of the government's budget is made up of foreign aid. More than four decades after political independence, the country still relies heavily on handouts from other countries, even though it is uniquely blessed with natural resources. Because we are so dependent, the donor nations influence and even dictate a lot of decisions that are made by our politicians and bureaucrats.

In the same way that the country is economically dependent and to some extent dictated to, individuals who work for other people are financially dependent and are dictated to by the people they work for. The employees may think that they are independent because they have been to school and have a job, but if you really think about it, they are financially dependent on the employer's pay cheque. They cannot survive without a job. It is their only source of income and livelihood.

People become financially independent when they work for themselves. They are able to stand on their own feet. And because of that, they cut off all kinds of domination and control. They become free from working for other people. But that does not mean that they are free from working for money. They are independent, but not free. True freedom is financial freedom.

WHAT FINANCIAL FREEDOM IS

Financial freedom means you do not have to work for money at all, either for someone else or for yourself, but are able to life your preferred lifestyle. You may work if you *want to*, but you do not *need to*. That is the ultimate lifestyle. It means you come to a point in life where you stop working and really begin to enjoy what life has to offer.

You come to a place of freedom when you have one or several sources of income which provide you enough to meet all your living expenses and do whatever else you want to do, without you expending your physical strength for it. Do you think there is such a place? Yes! Certainly! Definitely!

Let me give you a couple of examples. A friend of mine owns a business which employs people who do all the work without him having to be present all the time. He has established management and financial systems which operate on their own so he does not have to be there for the business to run. He only calls into the office once in a while. He spends most of his time with his wife and children. And when his friends are free, he is at the golf course. He has already taken his family on several overseas trips. He can do these things because he is financially free.

His business is making money for him even as he flies across the continents in the aeroplane. His investments make money for him twenty-four hours a day, including public holidays and even on a Sunday while he is in church or out on a picnic with his family.

Another friend owns several units which he rents out. Income from the rentals is sufficient to meet his mortgage obligations with the bank and other costs as well as his living expenses. He is financially free too. He does not need to work, but does so, because he enjoys the job. In addition to that, his plan is to combine part of his income from the job with income from the flats to buy several more rental units so that one day the rental income from these properties will enable him to do the things he really loves doing.

MOST WORKING PEOPLE HATE THEIR JOBS!

Most working people do not like to work, and some even hate their jobs. When they first got employed, they were very excited. Several people have confessed to me that they could not sleep the night before the interview and the first day at work. Their minds went into overdrive when they imagined the good things they would have as a result of getting jobs.

But as time passes and a job becomes routine and monotonous, people begin to lose that initial level of excitement and zeal. After a few years, they actually begin to hate their jobs, because most jobs are boring. They do the same things day in and day out to such a point that it becomes second nature to them. There are no challenges, and the pay remains the same for years.

But they *have to work*, because they have living expenses to meet. They have school fees to pay, for instance. So they get up every morning and go to work, trade their knowledge, talents, skills and strength all day for their employer's benefit, and come home tired and worn out each afternoon. They look forward to the weekends, public holidays and their annual leave, when they can sleep as long as they want to or do whatever gives them joy. They look forward to Friday afternoons and hate getting up on Monday mornings. A large number of them rush to nightclubs on Friday nights and drink and dance the night away in attempts to get the pressures of work off their shoulders and minds. Some go on binge drinking all weekend and stagger home late on Sunday nights.

But they have to get up and rush off to the office before eight o'clock on Monday and every other working day, because if they stop working, the money will stop coming in. Even if people do not express it openly, deep inside them, they wish they did not have to work but still have money to live on. If you have never worked for a salary, you will not know what I am talking about. A working person reading this can identify totally with what I am saying.

I suggest to you that hating your job is a yearning for financial freedom, when you can stop working and start enjoying life. The desire for freedom is in all of us. I feel it many times even though I am financially independent. Sometimes I just stay at home and read all day, and I desire to continue doing that every other day. But I cannot, because I need to work. I look forward to the day when I will be free from working for myself.

This desire for freedom drives me forward to do the things I do for a living. For instance, it drives to me write more books. I have written over 10 so far. My goal is to write at least 25 books. Then hopefully I can live off the residual income from the books once they are published.

Like the two friends I have made reference to above, many people in the world have reached that level of freedom. The bulk of the population however continues to work at their jobs. In fact, most people work for fortnightly or monthly pay all their lives until they reach retirement and old age. They work for their employer until their hair goes grey. A job is their only lifeline. They know of no other way.

MOST EMPLOYEES ARE HIGHLY INDEBTED

Debt is one thing that keep employees strapped to their jobs all their lives too. Most employees are indebted to banks, finance companies and informal money lenders–also known as loan sharks. Salaried people normally do not manage their income because of the mentality that 'next payday is coming.' They misuse their money, then when needs such as school fees or some emergencies arise, they run to the money lenders, using their jobs and superannuation savings as their security for the loans. Then because they have debts, they cling to their jobs for life support.

The sad thing is that once people start getting into debt, they find it easier to borrow money. The moment they establish some sort of track record with the lenders, borrowing becomes very convenient. So they borrow again and again until it becomes habitual. Debt then becomes a permanent part of their lives, and a lifestyle propped up by borrowed money passes on to the next generation, because all the while their children are learning money management by watching what their parents do.

When debt becomes habitual, employees end up working for the government (by paying their income taxes), their lenders, and the people who they buy their daily necessities from. This then becomes their routine: Go to work, get paid, pay taxes, repay debt, pay bills, and return to work. They become entangled in a 'vicious circle' from which they find it hard to break free.

A JOB CAN BECOME A STEPPING STONE TO INDEPENDENCE AND FREEDOM

Don't get me wrong. I am not against you having a paid job. One good thing about a paid job is that it provides you with income which you can save and invest to get yourself out of depending on the pay cheque. A job can become a transit point in your journey towards financial independence and freedom. But it needs a lot of self-control when it comes to handling money. Sadly, most employees do not exercise a high level of control over their spending habits.

I tell people in my church that what they hold in their hands after having given their tithes and offerings from the income they receive from their jobs can be classified into two groups. One is "food," and the other is "seed." What they spend for normal living is "food." This includes shopping, clothing, utilities, transport, school fees, etc.

But they should also convert some of their income into "seed," which is money they deliberately set aside or save for investment purposes. I tell them that a job is a "seed-source." It provides a source of seed which they can sow in order to become financially independent and free someday.

I tell people to become *seed-minded* and not to consider all their income as food to be eaten up. They must not be entirely *need-minded*. I am glad to say that many people have taken this message seriously and have started doing something with their income. I can see them not needing a pay cheque in the near future.

The point is this: A job can become a stepping stone towards you becoming financially independent and free, if you use your pay wisely. But ultimately, if you want to become financially independent and free, a job will not provide you that. Only your own business can give you true independence and freedom.

REASON # 7

GAIN CONTROL OVER TIME, ONE OF OUR MOST VALUABLE RESOURCES

AS I HAVE stated above, the majority of working people hate going to work, because they know there are better things they could do if they had to time to do it.

In America, for instance, it has been found that 90% of working class people hate their jobs. I believe this is representative of working people all over the world. They wish they could stay at home and do the things they enjoy doing. The more time they spend at work, the less they have for family or to go to some exotic places and relax.

What I am saying is this: Free time is valuable. Working at a job does not provide the amount of free time most people desire.

EMPLOYERS BUY TIME

When you work for someone else, you are really selling your time, skills, knowledge and expertise to that person. He pays you through a salary and other incentives. *As long as you are on his payroll, your time belongs to him.* He has bought your time. The amount of time he has to accomplish his goals is multiplied by the number of people he employs, including yours. If you consider that life is measured in time, the employer effectively owns part of your life! *You have literally sold yourself to him!*

When you graduate from school, you enter the job market. For employees, the job market is a place where they go out in search of jobs, in other words, opportunities to sell their time and skills. For the employers, it is a market where they are looking to buy time and skills. In many ways it is something like the slave markets of old, where slave masters went to buy slaves.

If you think this is not the case, ponder this: Every working day from eight to five o'clock, you cannot do anything or go anywhere you desire without your boss's permission. When he says, "Go," you go, and when he says "Come," you come. In other words, eight hours of every day–and hence eight hours of your life every working day–is under the employer's control.

And he pays you only a small proportion of what you make for him. He owns the capital and the system which makes up the organisation. You combine your energy, time and expertise with his system to make money for him. He determines how much you will receive for your efforts. Usually he keeps more for himself than he pays you.

Imagine if you used the whole eight hours each day working for yourself, and benefiting 100% from it. Could you make more than you are making every fortnight? I propose to you that the answer is "Yes."

THE HARDER YOU WORK FOR OTHERS, THE LESS TIME YOU HAVE FOR YOURSELF

When you work for others, the harder you work, the higher you may rise up the corporate ladder through promotion. But the higher you rise up the ladder, the busier you become, because you have more work to do and more people to supervise. Your responsibilities increase.

For instance, you might be the first person to come into the office and the last to leave each day. You might need to work weekends for free too, just because time on working days is insufficient. You have deadlines to meet. You want to please your boss so that hopefully he recognizes your efforts and pays a bonus at the end of the year or even a pay rise.

When you are busy with work, you will have less free time. And because you are so busy minding your employer's business, you will not have the time to think about doing something for yourself, not even do things like spending time with your children. You will be busy minding your employer's business that you will not have any time to mind your own.

Your employer will also make your life comfortable by providing all kinds of incentives and perks like rent-free accommodation, company vehicles, school fees, gratuity payments, commissions and bonuses which you will fear losing if you slow down. He may also give you high-sounding titles such as "supervisor," "manager" or even "chief executive officer." So you will work harder and harder to maintain your status as well as to rise even higher.

PUBLIC SUCCESS, PRIVATE FAILURE

You will not realize that the more successful you become, the less free time you have to be with your family. This is a true statement which is borne out by actual experience.

Most successful working people take off for the office early in the morning and come home very late. They spend the day taking care of their employers' businesses and come home tired and worn out. All they want to do after work is to take a cold shower, rest by watching TV, eat and sleep. When their spouses and children attempt to talk with them, their body language makes it evident that they are not in the mood to talk. The next day they get up and off they rush to work again.

This becomes their routine. They do it over and over until it becomes habitual. One consequence is that communication in the family breaks down, to a point where the children feel that the parents—and fathers in particular—have no interest in them. They therefore look for guidance and understanding elsewhere, particularly on the streets. It is probably true to say that an increasing number of young people who come face to face with the law are children of seemingly successful people.

The reason is that the parents are too busy minding other peoples' business that they neglect one of their primary businesses, which is to raise law-abiding and productive members of society. They are seemingly successful in the eyes of the public, but their homes are in a mess. *They become public successes but private failures.*

BUSINESS: A WAY TO TAKE CONTROL OF AND MULTIPLY YOUR TIME

Business is all about taking control of your time and multiplying it. You take control when you free yourself from your employer, and you multiply it by employing other people.

In business, the first few years might require a lot of your personal time and attention. You might need to work both day and night, during weekends and holidays. And what you do may not succeed at all. The experience all over the world is that 90% of businesses fail in the first five years, so yours could be one of those that fails.

However, if your business is successful and you have an efficient system in operation which does not require your daily oversight, after some time you do not need to be physically present for things to work. Your managers, supervisors and employees will do the work, with you only checking on things from time to time.

Your time will be multiplied by the number of people you employ. One of your employees could be driving and making deliveries, while someone else keeps the books. Someone supervises the work, while someone does the banking. It will be as if you have become omnipresent, being in different places and doing several things at the same time.

This process will definitely take time. It may be several years, or it may be ten or twenty years, depending on your area of business, your ability to persevere against setbacks, your ability to manage your finances, the quality of staff you employ, etc.

The system will operate on its own without your personal presence. Then you will have plenty of free time to do what you want. You may take your family for a trip to the Holy Land, attend a week-long church conference or spend some time in the village doing the fun things you used to do when you were a child. By the time you return, there will be money in your account. That sounds good, doesn't it?

BEING YOUR OWN BOSS BUYS TIME TO LOOK FOR MORE OPPORTUNITIES

When you work for somebody else, all your mental capacities and time are taken up caring for the employer's business. For instance, if you are an accountant, you spend most of your time at work literally counting your employer's money and ensuring that his books are in order. You do not have the time to think of anything for yourself.

When you work for yourself, you firstly *free your time*. Then the moment you start employing other people, you *multiply* the amount of time available to you. You will now be in a position to look for business and investment opportunities which provide better returns on your money.

I am convinced that business has the potential to provide you both the time and the money to invest in more businesses, and accelerate your progress towards financial freedom.

That is actually how the rich get richer. They spend time establishing a business, which is really another word for 'money printing machine.' Once the 'machine' is operating, they free their time to look for more cash-generating opportunities while those who work for their system mind it on a day to day basis.

I once met an acquaintance in town. When we shook hands, he let out a huge sigh of relief with a big smile on his face. I asked him what the good news was, and he told me that he had just resigned from his job. I shook hands with him again and said, "Welcome to real life."

He told me that he had a business which was run by his wife and several employees. As the business had grown, one part of him wanted to concentrate more time and energy attending to the needs of his business, but he could not because he had to look after the employer's interests. Many times when the circumstances were such that he just had to attend to the needs of his business, he would feel very guilty about using his employer's time to do his own thing. He felt torn in between.

He also knew that he could grow his business if he gave his full attention. So he had made the decision to resign his job. By resigning, he had taken back control over his time, and he felt completely free and relieved. He could now pursue his personal and business interests without having anyone to answer to. He had finally become his own boss.

REASON # 8

GAIN CONTROL OVER INCOME, TAX AND LIFE

LIFE IS FULL of surprises. We can have our plans but we do not have any control over what actually happens in our lives. Sometimes things work out the way we have planned; most times however, life does not work out as we would have liked.

There are no guarantees in life. But sometimes the way people treat us can make us feel that we have a secure future. For example, the way employers treat employees makes most employees think that their jobs are safe. The truth is that employees generally have no control over their jobs, their income, the tax they pay, and therefore their lives.

EMPLOYEES HAVE NO CONTROL OVER THEIR JOBS

If you really think about it, employees really do not have any control over their jobs. Even managers have no control over the positions in the organisations they manage. Control over each position is in the hands of the owners. But under certain circumstances even the owners lose control to others, such as banks and financial institutions.

As I have related, twice in my life I learnt the fact that I did not have control over my job. In the first instance, what we the employees did not know was that the company owners and managers had mortgaged the company's assets to the Westpac Bank. Control over the company's, and hence the employees', future was in the hand of the bank, not even the owners. When the bank realized that it could sell off assets and recoup what the company owed, it went ahead and did just that. It did not need the permission of the owners and managers to do so. We employees certainly did not have any say in the bank's decision.

In the second instance, the company owner, who had started the company from nothing and hence owned every position in the organisation, decided that my services were no longer required. That decision affected the commitments I had made on the assumption that I had an employment contract and that I was well covered at least over the next three years.

My commitments related to school fees and accommodation. I had assured the school that my children's fees would be paid by the employer, as stated in my employment contract. I had also assured the owners of the house we were living in that the employer would pay the monthly rental. I lost control of these commitments when I lost control of the job. Luckily I did not have any debts at that time, otherwise I would have lost the things I had bought with borrowed money or ended up in the courts with the debtors.

I have witnessed several retrenchment exercises being

carried out by one of the organisations I worked for. Fortunately I was not affected, but many other employees saw their jobs vanishing literally overnight. I have seen mature people crying like babies, and I have cried with them in empathy. I have bumped into several of these people later in other parts of the country, and I have felt sorry for them because their physical appearances had changed since the last time I saw them. Most have lost weight and many have aged fast and grown grey hair.

Employees do not have any control over their jobs. Just think about this for a moment: If your employer decided to terminate you tomorrow, what would you do? You could take a court injunction preventing the employer from sacking you, as people have been increasingly doing. You could accept the termination and seek court interpretation over the legality of the employer's decision. You could beg and cry for the employer to reverse his decision. If the person who made the decision is a manager, you could pay them a large bribe to change their mind, or even threaten them with physical violence, as some people do. Or if you are a public servant, you could talk to your Member of Parliament to apply political pressure on your boss to retain you.

But the fact would remain: *You would still not have any control over your job.* By taking any of the above actions you would simply delay or postpone the day of reckoning, but the day would come eventually.

Compare that with those who are in business for themselves. Things can happen which result in them losing their businesses. That is possible. But generally those who work for themselves have control over their source of income and livelihood. And as we have seen, nobody can sack a self-employed person because he is the boss.

EMPLOYEES HAVE NO CONTROL OVER WHEN THEY PAY THEIR TAXES AND HOW MUCH

This point is discussed more fully in Chapter 17. Suffice it to say that employees' income taxes are deducted from their pay directly by their employers. They pay tax before they meet all their living expenses. The amounts are even fixed, depending on salary level and other taxable benefits. And the tax rates are high as well.

Contrast that with self-employed people who have some control over when they pay their taxes, and how much. They can minimize their taxes, and they can even avoid paying taxes under certain conditions. For instance, someone who operates a PMV service or a trade store does not pay any income tax. Those who operate under companies pay at the end of the year, and that only if they have made a profit.

EMPLOYEES HAVE NO CONTROL OVER THEIR LIVES

Being an employee means that the best time of each day, week, month and year is under the control of the employer. And since life is counted in time, employees' lives are really under the control of their employers.

Even *where employees live* is controlled by the employers. I lived in one town for 22 years. I held three paid jobs over ten years of this period. Fortunately, all the employers I worked for were based in this town so we did not have to move.

Over this period I saw so many people transfer out to other centres at the command of their employers. Many of these people were very close family friends and church members. We wept with each other when they had to leave for other parts of the country, but cry is all we could do. As much as we would have liked to stay together for longer, there was nothing we could do. When the bosses decided, our friends–the employees–had to move, otherwise they would lose their jobs.

In some of these cases, I saw employers directing their employees to move at very short notice. They did not give the employees time to sort out their children's education or other personal and family matters. Employers did not seem to have considered the interests of the employees. They put their interests ahead of the employees', because they controlled the employees' lives.

Every time a family had to move, I was reminded over and over about the extent of control employers have over their employees. The employers can go as far as dictating where their employees live, even if the employees do not like it!

If you have been terminated, suspended, retrenched or transferred by your employer against your will, I know that you will agree with what I am saying. If you have not experienced any of these yet, I think you will still agree that as an employee, your life is in the control of the employer.

By controlling income through the pay cheque, employers gain control over their employees' livelihoods. To some extent employers dictate:

- What the employees eat (the better the pay, generally the better the food, and vice versa);
- What type of houses employees live in (if in fact accommodation is provided or housing allowances are paid);
- What the employees wear (again the better the pay, generally the better the clothing);
- Where and when the employees go for holidays;
- What schools the employees' children attend (and hence the quality of the education they receive); and
- Whether the employees travel by private or public transport.

That is a lot of areas of life employees yield to their employers. Is that the kind of life you want to live? I don't.

EMPLOYEES ARE LIKE PUPPETS

If you have watched a puppet show, you will have seen puppets of different shapes, sizes, and colours seemingly talking, singing, and dancing. What you have not seen is the fact that behind the curtain are people who pull strings or manipulate the puppets to make them do different things at the whim of the puppeteers. These people are actually in control of what the puppets seemingly say and do of their own accord.

You may not like me saying this, but people who work for others are really puppets to their employers. They get directions from the employers, who are really in control of their lives. When the employers pull strings, the employees move. *When the employers sing, the employees dance to the music.*

NOBODY DICTATES TO THE SELF-EMPLOYED

Compare that with people who are run their own businesses. Their time, and hence their lives, are entirely in their own hands. Nobody dictates when they work and when they rest. They decide where they live. They move at their own will, depending on where business opportunities lie. And they decide what they want to eat, what they want to wear, and they determine where they go for holidays, and which schools their children go to. They are their own bosses.

REASON # 9

LEVERAGE OTHER PEOPLES' TIME AND SKILLS TO GET AHEAD

WHAT IS LEVERAGE?

LEVERAGE IS A scientific term which comes from the fields of physics and mechanics. A lever is defined as "an object that is used with a pivotal point to multiply the mechanical force that can be applied to another object." The lever allows less effort to be expended to move an object a greater distance, or to lift up a heavy object with less physical strength.

Look at the following illustration. Lifting a box weighing 1,000 kilograms or one metric ton would probably be impossible for the average person. But using a lever, even a kid can move it with relative ease. By applying downward pressure on the lever, the box can be lifted upwards more easily than if somebody tried to lift it with their hands.

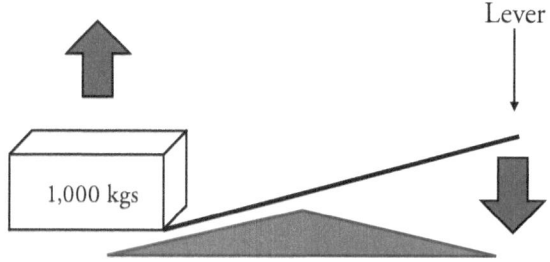

Leverage provides the person who has and uses it, to go further, do more, and achieve much with less effort. Let me explain this concept with several examples.

USING A ROPE AS LEVERAGE

Imagine that two vehicles are stuck in the mud. The driver of Vehicle "A" tries to press the accelerator pedal in an attempt to get the vehicle unstuck, while the driver of Vehicle "B" gets a group of boys to pull the vehicle with a rope while he steps lightly on the accelerator pedal. Which vehicle do you think would get out of the mud easily?

It is obvious that the vehicle which receives the pull has a much better chance. The driver does not need to exert much pressure. The driver of Vehicle "A" would see a lot of mud flying all over the place but make no progress. There would be a lot of commotion and fuel consumption. He would be stepping on the pedal, the vehicle would be making a lot of noise, the wheels would be turning furiously, and the mud would be flying, but the vehicle would not move forward as easily.

The rope and the boys pulling Vehicle "B" in this example are a form of leverage. They make it easy for the vehicle to become unstuck. There is not a lot of struggle like the other vehicle.

LEVERAGING DIFFERENT MEANS OF TRANSPORT

What has happened in the area of human transport exemplifies leverage. Initially, man's only form of transportation was walking. When man walked, he could only go so far as his legs could carry him in any given time. Later he learnt to domesticate and use animals such as horses, mules and donkeys, both to ride on the animal's backs and to get them to pull carriages in which he rode.

With the use of animal power he could travel far and faster than he could walk. Then came the motor car. With this form of leverage he could go even further within a short time than animals could carry him.

Later, man developed the aeroplane with which he could leave the surface of the earth and fly in the air like the birds. Today, with the supersonic jet, man can fly faster and go much further than any bird can go.

Earlier, animals such as horses and birds could travel faster and further than man. Today, due to the leverage of various means of transport, man can go faster and further than the birds and horses. Animals and birds are stuck with using their physical strength, as they have always done from the dawn of life. On the other hand, man, being more intelligent, imaginative and creative, has learnt to invent different means of transport to suit his need for faster travel.

On the seas man used the raft and the canoe, which he

paddled with his own strength. Later he learnt about the power of the wind, and developed the sail boat. He only had to arrange the sails, and let the wind blow him in any direction he wished to go. Then came steam boats, which he could steer wherever he wanted to go, and at faster speeds. Later came the diesel engine and the motor, which enabled man to travel much faster and further than the fish of the sea. So using these forms of leverage man has learnt to travel further on water with less effort over the years.

LEVERAGING DIFFERENT MEANS OF COMMUNICATION

In communication, man has gone from shouting messages to taming pigeons to carry messages, to using telephones, telexes, faxes and electronic mail (email). The introduction and availability of digital phones has changed the communication landscape forever.

In terms of writing, man has gone from the ink and feather to the ball point pen to typewriters, and now the personal computer.

LEVERAGING THE INTERNET

The Internet has become a very powerful form of leverage in today's knowledge- and information-driven economy. It has enabled millions of people from all walks of life to express their creativity and become ultra-rich. For instance, today, an increasing number of high school students are becoming millionaires through using the Internet. Millions of businesses are using the Internet to sell their products to a worldwide customer base. Such businesses are open on a 24/7 basis (24 hours a day, 7 days a week).

We are living in the Information Age. You can become a self-taught expert on any subject by browsing the World Wide Web and getting educated using the free information that is available from millions of websites. It is now easy to receive a university education from the comfort of your home over the Internet.

LEVERAGING THE BANK'S MONEY

Did you know that you can gain control of a K100,000 property by putting up only K20,000? Yes, you can. This is another form of leverage. If you want to buy such a property, the bank requires you to put up only 20% of the cost, and it will lend you 80%. So you use your K20,000 (a small amount) as leverage to get the bank's K80,000 (a large amount).

After you purchase the house, the bank only requires you to repay its loan at the agreed rate every month until the loan is extinguished. If you earn more from renting the house than the cost of the mortgage and other expenses related with owning the property, you make a return on your initial outlay of K20,000.

Let me give you an example of this form of leverage. Assume that you rent the property out at K2,000 per month. Your mortgage and maintenance costs are K1,800 per month. This leaves you with K200 at the end of each month. The return on your investment would be 12% (that is, K200 x 12 months = K2,400 ÷ K20,000 x 100). This rate of return would normally be better than what you could make by depositing K20,000 in a savings or interest-bearing account.

So essentially you have control over a K100,000 property which you can take ownership of when you repay the bank in full. In the meantime you realize a good return on your investment of K20,000.

There is another benefit which leveraging the bank's money also empowers you to realize. This has to do with the capital gains on the property. If the property increases in value over time, say to K150,000, the bank will not ask you for a share of the K50,000 increase in its market value. It is all yours, even though the bank has put up 80% of its initial value. The bank would be happy so long as you faithfully pay the agreed monthly amount.

You can also cash that amount if you want to, and the bank will give it to you. Or if you wanted to, you could use that K50,000 as equity to buy a second property worth K150,000.

If you want to start a business worth K100,000 and you have K50,000 only, the bank might lend you K50,000. In that way you use your K50,000 to start and own a business worth K100,000. These are powerful forms of financial leverage.

You can leverage your skills. You can also leverage your contacts and relationships to get ahead. Remember my story about using my relationship with the owner of the stationery shop to print my training notes on credit? That was a form of leverage.

I am sure that you can think of many more examples of leverage. The point is that life has become easier as man has developed various means of traveling faster and further, and doing more with less effort. In other words, the more leverage, the easier life has become.

HOW LEVERAGE OPERATES FOR THE SELF-EMPLOYED

How does this concept relate to self-employment and work? When you relate this to being your own boss, it will become obvious that people and their time, strength, expertise, and knowledge are forms of leverage which you can use to your advantage. You do not need to know everything and possess all the skills required by your business. You do not have to be a jack-of-all-trades. You can always buy what you lack from others by becoming an employer.

A friend of mine once started a fast food outlet, and he did not know a thing about cooking food. When he was renovating the shop, a young man approached him and asked if he could do the cooking. My friend had a look at the young man's papers and engaged him on the spot. In this case he did not need to know how to cook. He could avail himself of the young man's knowledge and skills by paying him a salary.

Another friend operates a vehicle repair shop through which he employs several tradesman mechanics and a panel beater. The guy is an Agriculture College graduate who has received no training whatsoever in motor mechanics. But he leverages his money to get trained and experienced mechanics to fix vehicles for his clients.

EMPLOYERS LEVERAGE OTHER PEOPLES' SKILLS TO GET AHEAD

Did you know that employers use their employees as their leverage to get ahead? Employers multiply their time by buying their employees' time. They multiply and increase the variety of the skills available to them by employing people with different skills.

What does this mean? It means that when you become an employee, you are being used by your employer. You are his lever. He is using you to go far and accomplish much with little effort on his part. This may be a crude way of putting it, but if you really think about it, there is a lot of truth to it.

I am not saying that it is bad for employers to ride on their employees' time, knowledge and skills to get ahead. I am merely opening your mind to see what you may not have been able to realize up to now. You may think it is not right, but that is the way the world operates.

YOU TOO CAN LEVERAGE OTHER PEOPLES' RESOURCES

My purpose in making this point is to get you to see that you too can leverage other people's resources if you become self-employed. In the beginning it might just be you and your spouse and family doing everything. But soon, it will become possible to buy other peoples' time and skills. They will do more and more, while you do less and less. And do you know who will benefit the most from the employees' efforts? You, the employer!

As the boss, you will pay the employees less than what they make for you. And the more employees you have, the more you will make. It might turn out that you have several employees whose total wages you can pay from the efforts of only one or two of them. You pocket what the rest of the employees produce.

BEING AN EMPLOYER IS A NOBLE THING

In case you feel guilty about buying and using other people's time and skills to get ahead financially, let me assure you that employing people is not a bad thing. On the contrary, it is a noble act.

After all, you would be providing employment, and in doing so, enabling your employees to sustain their lives and the lives of those who depend on them. You would be contributing to alleviating the unemployment problem facing the country. You would be part of the solution and not the problem.

How does that sound to you? I propose to you that the power of leverage is another reason why you need to seriously think about being your own boss one day.

REASON # 10

CONTRIBUTE TO JOB CREATION

I HAVE ALREADY DISCUSSED in Chapter 1 the fact that paid jobs are scarce today. There are too many people looking for jobs compared to the number of working age people. Unemployment is a major problem for the people, and a major challenge to the government.

We normally tend to criticise the government a lot about not creating jobs, but what I would like to bring out in this chapter is the fact that creating jobs is not a responsibility for government alone. Every citizen has the responsibility to create and provide jobs to others.

I believe that instead of blaming the government, we each have to ask ourselves what we are doing to address the problem. As President John F. Kennedy of the United States stated in his inaugural address, *"Ask not what your country can do for you, but what you can do for your country."* The government and the private sector are doing everything to create jobs; it is time for individual citizens such as you to make your contribution.

ONE PERSON OFF THE STREETS IS BETTER THAN ONE MORE ON THE STREETS

How can you as an individual contribute to alleviating the country's unemployment problem? I would like to propose to you that business is the way you can make a significant contribution.

If you are working and you become self-employed, you will immediately create one vacancy in the organisation you have been working for. It might mean that somebody else within the organisation takes your place, but ultimately it will mean one less person off the streets.

Look at it this way: Somebody takes your place, and somebody else takes his place, while another person is moved into the position previously occupied by the person who has replaced you. This process will continue until the last person in the organisation moves up, creating space for somebody new.

So when you leave an organisation to go into business, you start a chain reaction which ultimately leads to one person leaving the army of the unemployed. You will agree that one person off the streets is better than one more on the streets.

This is an important way to look at contributing personally, because I know that some people are protective of their jobs. They do not plan on letting go, and they do not want anyone coming close to their positions. They do not train other people, for instance, for fear that the people they train will take over their jobs. Some deliberately suppress their colleagues or subordinates and make them look bad in the eyes of senior management. They do not give room for others to rise up. They are like tall trees that enjoy all the sunshine and rain while the smaller trees underneath suffocate and wilt. They kill the morale of their subordinates, and provide them no sense of progress.

Some people have remained in their positions for many years without making any progress professionally or financially. They have remained in one position and performed certain functions for so long that they cling to these positions with both hands. They feel threatened by new recruits. They are really "dead wood" but they act and talk as if they are indispensable. I have seen many such people in government departments in particular. Such people should have left long ago and made way for younger, more energetic and productive people, but they hang on, and in doing so, fend off younger people.

I trust that you are not like these people. I trust that you are a person that cares for the success of others. I trust that you are willing to do what you can to empower others to succeed you. I trust that you are willing to groom other people and make way for them to replace you.

BUSINESS IS ABOUT CREATING JOBS

When you go into business, you have the possibility of creating jobs which many other people are desperately looking for. If your business grows and you become an employer, it will mean many people off the streets. Even if you engage people as casuals, cleaners or drivers, you will be contributing to alleviating the unemployment problem facing the country.

What would you like to do: Become part of the problem, or part of the solution? Getting into business means you become part of the answer to the problem of unemployment. We have too many people who are part of the problem. The country and the world needs more people who are part of the solution. We have too many employees already; we need more employers.

There are too many people looking for jobs. We need many job-creators, not job-seekers. Don't you think it is time you took risks, went into business, created jobs, and gave hope to others? I can guarantee that you will become a valued citizen of the country. You will also enjoy the satisfaction that comes with being a source of sustenance to other people.

When you get into business, your mind may focus on making as much money as you can, and thereby improving your living standard. But the big picture is that what you are doing is not only for your own good, but for many others as well. The more money you make, the more people you need for your business to grow further. When you employ people, you support many others who depend on each person who works for you. You can think of spouses, children and other family members. Seen this way, starting a business is a very noble act.

EMPLOYERS ENJOY MANY TAX ADVANTAGES

I discuss many tax advantages which are available to self-employed and business people in Chapters 17 and 18. Do you know why the government looks upon business people favourably when it comes to tax matters? It is because business people create jobs. The government looks upon them as its partners in providing jobs to the population. So it provides many incentives to business people, so that they can invest more and create more jobs.

But the government hits employees with high tax rates. It taxes them even before they get their pay into their hands. And it works closely with employers to ensure that employees pay every toea they are supposed to pay.

For businesses, the tax rates are lower. As well as that, the government allows business owners to pay tax at the end of the year, while employees are taxed at the end of each fortnight. It is as if the government cannot trust people who work for others, but trusts those who provide work to others.

REASON # 11

DEVELOP BETTER MONEY HABITS

ONE OF THE major differences between the employed and the self-employed is their attitude towards money. There are major differences in the thinking of people who are employed and those who are self-employed.

Self-employed people generally spend their money more prudently than those who receive regular pay. They are generally more imaginative and creative. They have no guarantee of future income, so they use what they have wisely. Not only that. They also think about what more they can do to increase their earnings. Their minds, eyes and ears are more open to opportunities around them than people who are focused on minding their employers' businesses.

THE EMPLOYED HAVE DIFFERENT MINDSETS FROM THE SELF-EMPLOYED

Unlike employed people whose dominant thinking is on how they can *work for money* and *spend money*, self-employed people think a lot about how they can *make money* and *make money work for them*. They use their imaginations to think about the needs of society, and come up with creative solutions. They might invent a completely new way of doing things, or they might make slight to significant improvements to existing methods or products. It is what these people do that brings improvements and advancement to society at large.

This is what entrepreneurship is all about. Entrepreneurs are people who use their imaginations to start businesses which seek to address some needs of society with a view to making life more convenient living. The majority of the world's entrepreneurs have been, and continue to be, business people. They are the people who take risks with their time, skills, expertise and money. When they succeed, many other people benefit by working for them.

THE SELF-EMPLOYED AND SUPERANNUATION

One factor which influences salaried people in the use of their money is the fact that they have savings in their accounts with superannuation funds. These funds have been set up by law to cater for the future of working people because most of them, if given the chance, will spend everything without any savings for their future. The funds have also been established with the recognition that one day all employees will have to retire from work.

Super funds are really "forced savings" schemes. The government has set them up to force people to save. But the problem is generally that because people have savings in the funds which their employers also contribute to, they think their future is secure, so they normally spend what they earn with a great deal of carelessness.

Self-employed people generally know that their future is insecure, because many of them do not contribute to super funds. They therefore manage their money with the future in mind. The lack of security over their future needs forces them to think about providing for the future with what they have at present.

In Papua New Guinea the National Superannuation Fund (Nasfund) introduced a superannuation scheme for the self-employed in October 2006 called *Eda Supa*. The scheme is aimed at encouraging people who work for themselves to save for their future. There will be no employers' contributions, and contributors are not obliged to make regular (i.e. fortnightly or monthly) deposits, in recognition of the fact that income earned by self-employed people is irregular.

The scheme may be good, but I fear that it might have the effect of dampening the enthusiasm of the self-employed people to use their money creatively and efficiently. Knowing that they have savings might engender a sense of complacency and security which might work against them being creative with their money.

In my opinion, whether self-employed people participate in the scheme will depend on the rate of return they expect to earn from the super fund as opposed to what they can earn if they reinvested their money into their own businesses rather than hand it over to the fund.

Many self-employed people are not that academically qualified, but they exercise a lot of common sense when it comes to their money habits. One of that common sense ways of looking at money is the rate of return. They always have some crude sense of the returns they can realize from different ventures. They will compare the benefits they perceive from saving in a super fund to investing the money in other ventures. If they judge that they can get better returns from investing their money themselves than the returns they expect to get from the super fund, they will simply not save with the super fund.

THE TIME VALUE OF MONEY

One of the most important concepts in the world of finance is that of *"the time value of money."* This concept simply says that *"a Kina today is better than a Kina tomorrow."* In other words, the earning potential of what you have in your hands today is greater than what you expect to receive in future. Why? Because if you invest what you have today or this year, and you will have more tomorrow or next year. You can certainly buy more today than next year due to inflation.

What you expect to earn tomorrow or at any time in future is uncertain due to two factors. Firstly, there is no guarantee that you will actually earn what you expect in future. You might get sacked this afternoon or die tonight. Secondly, the *present value of future earnings* is lower than that of money you have in your hands today.

Let me explain this second point.

THE PRESENT VALUE OF FUTURE EARNINGS

If the interest rate on bank deposits is 5% per annum and you placed K1,000 in an interest-bearing account today, in a year's time your money will earn K50 interest [K1,000 x 0.05]. That is why it is better for you to have K1,000 today.

On the other hand, if you earned K1,000 in a year's time, and using the interest as the discount factor, that K1,000 would be worth only K952 today [K1,000 ÷ 1.05]. In other words, the *present value* of K1,000 in a year's time is K952. Most of us think that K1,000 next year is equal to K1,000 today, but this is not the case if we really understand the principles upon which money works.

Let us consider what this concept means for people who work for others on a three-year contract. Let us assume that you enter into an employment contract under which your total remuneration package is K100,000 per year for three years. What is important to you is how much that package is worth to you the moment you sign the contract. Is it really worth K300,000? You would think that it is, but it is not.

To determine the present value of the K300,000 you expect to earn over the next three years, you need to discount the cash flow of K100,000 per year with the bank's interest rate on deposits. If the interest rate is 5%, the present value of your employment package would be K259,151, not K300,000.

If the interest rate is 2%, the present value of the package would be be K282,697, and if the rate was 8%, the present value of the package would be K238,150. (Note: These calculations are derived from the formula for Present Value in the Microsoft Excel spreadsheet program).

What you will note is that the lower the interest rate (or discount factor) the higher the present value of an income stream, and vice versa. In other words, your three-year salary package will be closer to the value you sign a contract during periods when interest rates are low. But when the interest rate is high, the present value of your expected earnings decline. In other words, when interest rates are high, it is better for you to have K300,000 this year than to have it in lots of K100,000 per year over the next three years.

Self-employed people seem to understand these concepts better (even though they do not know their technical terms) than those who work for a salary. Salaried people usually look towards next payday (which is not worth the same today), while the self-employed focus on what they can do with what they have today.

Both the employed and the self-employed use their money with the future in mind, but their thinking about the future is completely different. The employed think about next payday. Their self-talk or internal dialogue goes something like this: *"I will save some money next payday."* Or, *"I will invest my leave pay in a part-time business."* The self-employed ask themselves, *"What can I do with the money I have today, so that I make more in the future?"*

Employed people think about what they will do with future earnings, while self-employed people think about what they will do with what they have today in a way that caters for the future. So although both think of the future, there is a major difference in how they see the future.

And the way they perceive the future dictates how they spend their money. Generally salaried people take comfort from the fact that income is regular, and such comfort makes them careless. They are always thinking about future earnings that they misuse current earnings. The self-employed on the other hand know that income is not regular, so they use money more wisely. It seems as if the more secure people are, the more careless they are with their money; and the less secure, the more prudent they are.

THE MONEY HABITS OF PUBLIC SECTOR EMPLOYEES

Let me also say something about the money habits of public sector employees, or those who work for the government. In government departments and agencies, people essentially get paid to spend money. The more money they spend, the bigger their organisations are, and the more people they need. If an organisation spends less in one year than it did the previous year (in other words, if the organization cuts costs and makes savings), it gets a budget cut the following year. If it does not spend everything, the balance goes back to consolidated revenue.

The organisation is said to lack capacity to absorb funds. So there is pressure to spend, spend, and spend. There is no reward or incentive for the organization that save public monies.

This is the culture within which the public servants operate. They get used to spending huge amounts of money without blinking. If the government runs out of money, it can always increase taxes, or borrow from the banks and international organisations such as the World Bank or Asian Development Bank.

When these people go home after work from this spending culture, they take this spending habit with them. So they treat their own money the same way they treat public monies.

Their money habits at work kick in, and they spend, spend, and spend, with the false sense of comfort that next payday will always come. They have the added sense of job security, knowing that their union will fight for them if the employer attempts to terminate or retrench them.

The flipside is also true. Public servants develop the spending habit at home and take it to work. They do not know how to spend their own money well. When they come to the work place, there are huge amounts of public monies available to them. Their personal money habits dominate their decisions, with the result that they spend without much thought.

This is probably why politicians are good at misusing public money. Most of them do not know how to spend their own money. Some even had no money to spend before becoming politicians. When they become MPs, suddenly they are confronted with the power to make decisions over millions of public funds. But because they have not inculcated good money habits in their lives, they are unable to exercise the needed level of prudence and discipline. So they go on spending sprees, even to the point of spending public monies for their individual benefit.

MOST PRIVATE SECTOR EMPLOYEES THROW FINANCIAL CONTROL OUT THE WINDOW

Private sector employees work in an environment where cost control and management are everyday issues they deal with. They are told over and over to cut costs and maximize profits.

But when it comes to personal finances, these people seem to throw control and discipline out the window.

Accountants and financial controllers are the worst offenders. You would think they would be the most financially successful and prosperous people, but most are not. They are some of the worst drunkards, gamblers, and debtors. Many seemingly successful economists, accountants, financial controllers and auditors are complete failures when it comes to managing their own money.

The same can be said of bankers too. They can see the power of saving and investing every day. Every day they deal with small business people. They advise these people on how they can invest their money or how to leverage the bank's money to get ahead by investing in real estate, for instance. But they themselves live in continual financial struggle. They tell business people to borrow for investment, but they themselves borrow for consumption. They advise people about how to buy and rent property but they themselves live in squatter settlements no matter how long they have worked in banks.

EMPLOYEES GENERALLY HAVE BAD MONEY HABITS

Employees, whether they work in the public or private sector, generally have bad money habits. Their attitude to money again is dictated by the regularity of the pay cheque. They usually spend their money with "next pay day" in mind. They are always thinking about what they will do in future that what they have in their hands slips out without them realizing it.

Self-employed people use their money with more discretion. They are generally better money managers. You do not have to be self-employed to become a better manager of your money. Some self-employed are bad money managers too. But when you become self-employed, the chances of you becoming better at managing your money are greater than when you work for other people.

I have met so many people engaged in informal business activities over the years. I have also met many people running formal or registered businesses. Generally, I have found such people to be more prudent money managers than the working class. The operating environments and cultures are definitely different.

REASON # 12

MAKE MONEY WORK FOR YOU RATHER THAN YOU WORKING FOR MONEY

IF YOU HAVE read my book *Life After Graduation*, you will know that before formal schools came into being, children learned from their parents at home. Formal schools came into being after the Industrial Revolution, when schools were introduced to teach and train people to work in factories, rail tracks, mines and offices.

SCHOOL TEACHES YOU TO WORK FOR MONEY

The education system still teaches students to work for others as employees. Even business schools teach people how to manage other peoples' businesses. There is no business college in Papua New Guinea that teaches its students how to start and run their own businesses.

So, given such training and programming, what do school-leavers do immediately upon graduation? Of course they do what they have been conditioned to do, which is to look for paid jobs. And what do they really do when they become employed? They work *for* money.

They get up each working day, take a shower, eat some breakfast (if they do at all), then rush to the office before the official starting time. After spending a whole day at work attending to their employers' businesses, they return home tired and worn out. After taking a shower, watching TV and eating, they go to bed. The next day they get up and repeat what they did the previous day. This is their routine all their working lives.

Most employees love Fridays and hate Sunday nights. They love Fridays because it is the end of another week. Payday Fridays are particularly exciting because they will get paid for working for the employers. Sunday nights and Monday mornings are not particularly exciting because they must get back to their normal routine.

Employees work for money. But the problem is that generally what they receive from their employers is either just enough to survive or to little compared with their needs. Most employers have an idea what it costs to live, so they pay at the cost of living. It is up to the employees to manage their pay in order to survive until next payday. Only a few employers pay more than what their employees need to live. The majority of employers pay the employees enough to keep them from leaving.

WORK IS BUSY-NESS MINDING OTHER PEOPLES' BUSINESS

Employees are so busy working for money that they do not learn anything about how money works. They make money and spend it, but have no time to sit down and really think about where they are actually heading. *Busy-ness* in looking after the affairs of their employers keeps them from thinking about being in *business* for themselves.

HOW TO MAKE MONEY WORK FOR YOU

Being in business is really about putting money to work for you. It is about harnessing money and engaging it as an employee. It is about making money work for you rather than you working for money.

There are several ways to engage money as an employee. One way is saving. When you save money in a bank account, the bank lends your money to borrowers. It charges the borrowers interest, then it pays you interest for using your money. The bank charges borrowers a higher interest than it pays you. So your money makes money through interest earnings. If you leave your money long enough, it will grow exponentially through the power of compounding.

But saving only makes money if the interest rate is higher than inflation and interest-withholding tax. During periods of low interest and high inflation, saving actually results in savers losing money instead of making it. As well as that, saving is a slow way of becoming financially independent and free.

Another way to employ money is to lend it. When you save money, you actually lend it to the bank. You can also lend money to the government by purchasing Treasury Bills and government bonds. Or if you invest money in a business, the Tax Office would treat your investment as a loan to the business. You can also lend money to other people, for example by becoming an informal money lender.

When you lend money in any of these ways, it becomes a good servant. It will bring back more money to you. But when you borrow money, it will become a terrible master. You will have to work hard to repay it with interest to the lender. Those who lend to you will wake up each morning richer, while you get up poorer.

You can also invest money in a business, a piece of real estate, or in the stock market. When you do that, it will bring you more money.

THE FIVE LAWS OF GOLD

I have quoted George Clasen's Five Laws of Gold in *Winning The Game Of Money*. For our present discussion, I feel that it is appropriate to quote the Five Laws again. Here they are:

> Law # 1: *Gold cometh gladly and in increasing quantity to any man who will put by not less than one-tenth of his earnings to create an estate for his future and that of his family.*
>
> [Anybody that saves at least 10 percent of his income on a consistent basis will eventually become wealthy.]
>
> Law # 2: *Gold laboureth diligently and contentedly for the wise owner who finds for it profitable*

employment, multiplying even as the flocks of the field.

[Money works and multiplies for the person that finds it a job, such as being put to work in a business.]

Law # 3: *Gold clingeth to the protection of the cautious owner who invests it under the advice of wise men in its handling.*

[This law encourages us to seek financial advice from knowledgeable and experienced people.]

Law # 4: *Gold slips away from the man who invests it in businesses or purposes with which he is not familiar or which are not approved by those skilled in its keeping.*

[This law says that if you do not understand the business or investment you are in, you will lose your money.]

Law # 5: *Gold flees the man who would force it to impossible earnings or who followeth the advice of tricksters and schemers or who trusts it to his own inexperience and romantic desires in investment.*

[Those who listen to promoters of fast-money

schemes will lose their money. Money will flee from such people.]

The second law is relevant to this chapter. It says that money is like a servant or employee. It works for the person that harnesses it and puts it to work.

Money is said to be a terrible master. The love for money drives people to do many things that are illegal and immoral. For instance, people steal, bribe and get bribed, pervert the course of justice, get divorced, kill, sell their bodies, sell drugs, etc, just to get money. The Bible actually says *the love for money is a root of all kinds of evil.*

But money can also become a faithful servant for those who are able to make it work for them. As a servant, money knows no rest. It works both day and night. It does not recognize weekends and public holidays. It works on a 24/7 basis. It does not become sick; it does not become old; and it does not die. And the harder it works, the more it multiplies. Money is the ideal employee. It reproduces itself over and over as time passes, such that its employer or boss can afford to take a life-long holiday.

BUSINESS IS ABOUT EMPLOYING MONEY

When you work for money, you do not learn much about making money work for you. You are so busy making money by trading your time and expertise, that you have no time to even think about making money work for you. When you become self-employed, you will have the time to think about how best to make money work for your benefit.

This is another powerful reason why you should think about being in business for yourself instead of working in somebody else's business. A business will empower you to take control of money and make it work for you as a servant. And it will serve you well.

REASON # 13

DEVELOP COST-CONSCIOUSNESS AND PROFIT-MINDEDNESS

DONALD TRUMP RELATES in *Why We Want You To Be Rich*, a book he co-authored with Robert Kiyosaki, that when he asked one of his staff to get a quote on a new set of chairs for one of his restaurants, the employee presented him with a quote of US$1,500 for each chair. Mr. Trump thought the chair was too pricey, so he made a few telephone calls himself and obtained a quote for a better, more comfortable chair, at only US$90 apiece.

You might wonder why a multi-billionaire like Mr. Trump would be fussy over such a tiny amount. He could have easily closed his eyes and written the cheque without even bothering to double check. But this story demonstrates the difference in mindset between employees and employers. It becomes easy for employees to spend money, because it does not cost them personally. But for the employers, cost reduction and profit maximization is foremost on their minds.

EMPLOYEES SPEND MONEY WITHOUT BLINKING

Employees can spend money if given the chance. And they usually go for the most expensive too. For example, if the company they work for wants to buy a vehicle, they would usually go for a fully-kitted Toyota instead of a relatively cheaper brand which can do the job equally well. Top public servants in Port Moresby would normally favour the latest Toyota VX Landcruiser, Hilux double-cab utility or ten-seater troop carrier, with tinted windows and mag wheels, stereo and air conditioning, when what they need are small town cars. They think comfort and style. After all, it does not cost them personally. They do not feel any pinch in the hip pocket.

Government bureaucrats can write cheques for hundreds of thousands or even millions without blinking. If they were spending out of their own personal accounts, they would shudder every time they lifted their pens to sign the cheques. But since somebody else (the tax payer) is paying the expenses, they can spend big amounts without second thought, all in the name of providing services to the public.

I have seen most employees burning fuel which their employers pay for by making unnecessary trips. They fill the fuel tank, take a trip and return empty. Many of the long trips are job-related, but most of the shorter trips within the places they visit are really unnecessary. If they had used their own vehicles and fuel, or if they hired the vehicles using their own money, they would not make so many small trips. They would be cost-conscious.

One of my friends owns a hire car company. I have seen company and government executives hiring these vehicles and using them recklessly, filling the vehicles with friends and taking them to the pubs etc, and even wrecking the vehicles. I have checked the backgrounds of a few of them and it has turned out that these people do not have their own cars. When they take trips to the provinces, it is their only chance to drive good vehicles. Their employers pay for the hire costs, so they misuse the vehicles. When they return to their places of employment, they go back to catching public transport to and from work.

Misuse of telephones is another area where employees are good at wasting their employers' time and money. Many calls are private in nature. And many genuine calls take longer than they should. People do not get to the point too. They tend to spend a few minutes greeting each other and exchanging news or gossip before getting down to business. And when talking business, they repeat things over and over without much thought for the employer who will pay the bill. Women are usually the worst offenders but men are equally guilty. People forget that the longer they are on the phone, the more somebody is going to pay for it.

I must admit I used to do this too when I worked for other people. But since becoming self-employed, I have been very careful on the phone. I try my best to get to the point as much as possible, because I know that the longer I talk unnecessarily, the more I will pay.

PUBLIC SERVANTS ARE NOT GOOD AT BUSINESS

The record of government-owned businesses is dismal all over the world. This is because such businesses employ public servants to manage them. The problem with public servants is that they are generally not good managers. They don't have the entrepreneurial mindset. The result is that businesses and projects managed by public servants generally end up losing rather than making money.

The managers are not profit-minded. They know that they can always request the government for financial support should the organizations run out of money. They also know that their own survival is not linked to performance and profitability, so there is no real pressure to minimize cost and maximize profit.

This is why most state-owned businesses the world over and particularly in Papua New Guinea have not made any money and have had to be supported annually by the government until recently, when several of them were corporatised and brought under professional management.

BUSINESS PEOPLE SPEND MONEY WITH ONE EYE ON THE "BOTTOM LINE"

Self-employed people and business owners are naturally cost-conscious. They always make spending decisions with one eye on their profit margin or "bottom line." They think "value for money" all the time. For instance, instead of a fully-kitted Toyota, they will go for a cheaper brand as long as it has the common features and can go from point "A" to point "B."

When I was employed, and occasionally when I have received short-term consulting assignments, I usually stayed in top hotels and used hire cars. Lately I have been doing a bit of traveling to sell my books. On these occasions, I have stayed at guesthouses and used taxis and public transport. I have even been conscious of the food I have eaten and the length of the calls I have made on my mobile phone. When it has not been absolutely necessary to talk with clients, I have communicated using text messages or email, and found these means to be just as effective.

When you work for yourself, you will be very conscious of the costs and benefits of all financial decisions that you make. You will keep the cost-benefit ratio of your decisions foremost in your mind.

Recently I made a trip to Port Moresby to follow up on several potential clients. It cost me about K1,100 for a return airline ticket plus about K500 in accommodation, transport and food.

When I arrived in the city, things did not seem to work out as I had anticipated, so I stood the chance of having spent money to make the trip without making any money in return. But I did not want to give up. I remember telling myself that I would sell some books to at least cover the cost of the trip.

The afternoon before the day I was to return, I called in to check on a last client. The shop was very busy and I had to wait for over three quarters of an hour before the manager came out. I expected him to tell me to come back some other time, but to my surprise he placed an order on the spot. The long wait was worthwhile, because the order was worth more than I had spent to make the trip, which he paid that same afternoon.

So I made money which I would not have made had I not made the trip. But more importantly, I managed to get my book on the buyer's bookshelf, which will stand me in good stead in future, because the client is a major book seller in the country. The returns for that trip and the long wait will be multiplied with each order the client places.

If I had gone to see the client on behalf of my employer, I would certainly have walked away after waiting for a few minutes. It would have been easy to give my employer the excuse that the client had been busy and I could not meet him this time around. Such an excuse would have given me reason to make another trip at the employer's expense.

This is actually what many employees do. They take a lot of unnecessary trips just to claim travel allowances, drive around in hire cars and sleep in hotels. Many take these trips more for the benefits to them personally than to promote the interests of their employers. Some of the business could be done more cheaply over the phone but they choose not to do it that way. They love to travel because the costs do not come out of their pockets.

In my case, because I had spent my own money, I had to make money to cover the cost of the trip as well as something additional. I became cost-conscious and profit-minded.

Being a self-published author means that I write and market my books all by myself. Only the printing is done by commercial printers. In selling books, I have found that you have to be willing to send out free copies to potential clients. Just writing letters to them informing them of your book will not make sales, because for most book buyers, seeing is believing.

Some clients whom I have sent copies of the books have not purchased even one book, while some have bought relatively large quantities. When I have factored in the cost of the free copies plus postage, one part of my mind has resisted the idea of giving free or complimentary copies to clients, and I have hesitated. But the other part of my mind has helped me see the free copies as an investment from which I can realize a return. And the rate of return on the investment of one book given away has been very high. For instance, recently I sent one copy to a bookshop and received an order for fifty copies. It cost me K25 to send the book (cost of printing one copy plus postage) and I made a net income of K1,800. That is a return of 7,100% on this transaction.

That is the kind of calculation going on in my mind every time I make a decision. And that is the mentality you will develop when you work for yourself. Every expense will become an investment from which you can expect returns. If there are no potential returns, you will not spend money. If you spend money, you must make money either immediately or in future.

REASON # 14

REALISE YOUR POTENTIAL

I HAVE RELATED THAT I became self-employed after searching unsuccessfully for a job for eight months. If you have never been faced with such a situation, you will not appreciate the mental and emotional pressures that are associated with not having a job and hence income on one hand, and seeing your living expenses and commitments such as school fees and house rent on the other. It is tormenting to see your kids watch other kids eat good food while they live on sweet potato and biscuits because their parents cannot afford to buy good food.

Today I can testify that the eight-month ordeal did us a lot of good. One important consideration for me is that if I had not been unemployed then, I would still be labouring for other people today. I would be using my time, talents, skills, knowledge and experience to make them rich at my expense.

I thank God for the pressure I went through then, which helped me to begin thinking about becoming self-employed. The prospect of getting evicted from the house we were living in, the children staying out of school and so on prompted me to really think hard about working for myself.

"Create Your Own Job If Nobody Gives You One" is the title to Chapter 11 of my book *Life After Graduation*. This title encapsulates the thoughts that came so forcefully to me at the time. The dominant thoughts were: *"You better create your own job because nobody will give you one."* In other words, create a job, not hunt for it.

In fact the manager of a coffee exporting company asked me what I was up to when I went to present the idea of conducting a training course. I remember answering him, *"I am trying to create my own job."* And I am glad I did.

NECESSITY IS THE MOTHER OF INVENTION

I had the potential to make a living apart from depending on a salary. But as long as I worked for my employers, my mind was closed to the possibility of working for myself. It did not even enter my mind at all that I could survive without a salary.

When the salary got cut off and there was no hope of getting another job, my mind began to go to work. I started thinking about who I was, what I had in my hands and life, what I could do with what I had, etc. It was during this period of contemplation that my hidden potential, which had lain dormant all along, began to stir. I did not realize that I could live without a salary until I was pushed to the corner. It is said that, *"Necessity is the mother of invention."* I can testify that this saying is true.

The potential to do something for yourself, or be your own boss, definitely lies in everyone. It was in your ancestors, all of whom were self-employed. And it is in you. But as long as you depend on a job, that potential will lie dormant. Your potential is alive but is sleeping. The shock that comes with getting terminated or not having a job can awaken it.

THE POTENTIAL OF HUMAN BEINGS

Do you want to know the potential all human beings have? Here is something I read in one of the handbooks put out by the Human Development Institute, which conducts Personal Viability courses throughout the country. It talks about the makeup and potential of each human being alive on the face of the earth:

> Your eyes contain a hundred million receptors so that you may see the wonders of the universe. Your ear contains 24,000 fibres to vibrate to the sounds of the universe. Your voice can speak and sing to the most creative tune. Your limbs can perform the most intricate movements with its 500 muscles, 200 bones, and 10 kilometres of nerve fibre all ready to work for your benefit.
>
> Your heart is the most advanced pump in creation. It pumps 36,000,000 beats, asleep or awake, pumping more than 2,500,000 litres of blood through more than 100,000 kilometres of veins, arteries and tubing each year.
>
> Your skin is a miracle itself. It does not rust. It constantly renews itself automatically, with old cells replaced by new.
>
> Your lungs filter the most poisonous gases

to give you life-supporting oxygen through 600,000,000 pockets of folded flesh.

Your blood is another marvel of creation. Your body has approximately 5 litres of blood which contains 22,000,000,000,000,000,000 blood cells and within each cell are millions of molecules and within each molecule an atom oscillating at more than 10,000,000 times each second. Each second, 2,000,000 of your blood cells die to be replaced by 2,000,000 more in a resurrection that has continued since birth.

Your brain is the most complex structure in the universe. Within its $1^{1/2}$ kilos are 13,000,000,000,000 nerve cells to help you store away every perception, sound, taste, smell and action you have experienced since birth. Within these nerve cells are more than 1,000,000,000,000,000 protein molecules. And to assist you control your body, there are 4,000,000 pain-sensitive structures, 500,000 touch detectors, and more than 200,000 temperature detectors.

No nation's wealth is better protected than your brain. No ancient wonder of the world is greater than you. You are the finest creation of all. Within you is enough atomic energy to destroy any city on earth and rebuild it again. You are unique. Never in all the seventy billion humans who have lived in this world since the beginning of time has there been anyone exactly like you. Never until the end of time will there be another like you.

You have powers unknown to any other creature in the universe. You have the power to think, love, will, laugh, imagine, create, plan, speak, act and pray. You are the ultimate creation who can adjust to any condition of climate, hardship, or challenge. You can find and manage your destiny, to become whatever you wish to be for you to have the greatest of all power that is the power to choose."

Wow! Think about what you really have in you, what you are made of–what makes you, you. The person who authored this has not exaggerated. What they have written is scientific fact about each one of us.

American psychologist Professor William James has said this:

> Compared with what we ought to be, we are only half awake. We are making use of only a small part of our physical and mental resources. Stating the thing broadly, the human individual lives far within his limits. He possesses powers of various sorts which he habitually fails to use.

Saint Augustine is said to have made this statement about human potential:

> Man travels hundreds of miles to gaze at the broad expanse of the ocean. He looks in awe

at the heavens above. He stares in wonderment at the trees and fields and mountains and the rivers and streams, and then he passes himself by without a thought. God's most amazing creation!

Ralph Waldo Emerson said:

What lies *behind* you and what lies *before* you pales into insignificance when compared to what lies *within* you.

What we can say is this: You have been designed for success; I have been designed for success; we all have been designed for success. Or as the Bible says, "*We have been fearfully and wonderfully created.*" Do not believe the evolutionists. We are not products of chance or of evolution. We did not come from monkeys. God created each one of us in His own image to live to the fullest as well as to live forever.

But even though all of us have the same make up regardless of the colour of our skin and cultural backgrounds, only a few succeed in realizing a greater measure of their potential while the majority throughout the world struggles all their lives. One of the main reasons for this is that most of us do not believe in ourselves. We live with an inferiority complex most of our lives. For example, many of us think that people from some parts of the world are more knowledgeable than our local people. We don't believe we can amount to anything.

Here is what Michael J. Lowe has stated in his book

Mission Possible about how our thoughts and beliefs affect how successful we are in life:

> If you are certain that something is impossible or beyond what you are capable of producing, your mind will immediately go into search mode to find reasons to support this particular belief... once a disempowering belief is entrenched within your subconscious mind, your brain will fail to even question its integrity. That is why so many people live within a prison of self-induced limitation. They are unaware of their own potential because they are prisoners of their databanks. Sadly, many people destroy their birthright of success because they consistently focus on what they cannot have or do, when the only thing actually worthy of their belief is why they can!

To realize a greater measure of your potential, a change in thinking is necessary. Books such as this can challenge you and open your mind to believing in yourself more.

POSITIVELY ENGINEERED, NEGATIVELY GEARED

One of my favourite sayings is:

> We are so positively engineered but are negatively geared.

I coined this statement when preaching a sermon in the church on being positive about life, and I have repeated it at many gatherings because it is so true.

We have been engineered, constructed and wired to live prosperous and successful lives, but we normally live in defeat mainly because of the way we perceive ourselves. Every time something happens, our minds quickly imagine the worst possible that could happen. We quickly shift into reverse gear. We are quick at jumping to conclusions which are adverse against ourselves. We become fearful and worried. We think loss. We think defeat. We think death. We think we cannot do much or be somebody. We normally think and size ourselves by what we have been in the past and what we are at present, not in terms of what we can be in the future.

Have you noticed that in your own life? I have, and I struggle to deliberately think positively. As a Christian, I know the Bible says that everything works for the good of those who love God and are called according to his purposes. This is a favourite verse for many people, but most of us struggle to see the good in every bad situation or circumstance. We usually focus and gaze at the negative so much that it overwhelms us.

Somebody defined fear as *"False evidence appearing real."* We look at something or hear something, and we immediately become afraid without really looking into it further to establish the truth or giving it time to mature and come to its conclusion.

Most of us are negatively geared in our minds. Our reactions to situations are driven a lot by negative mindsets and perceptions.

A study was carried out in the United States involving

thousands of people. Respondents were asked what their biggest fears were, or what worried them the most. A few months later the researchers returned and asked the same respondents whether what they had been worried about and feared had actually taken place. What they discovered was very interesting: *90% of the people responded that the bad things they had worried about did not take place.*

The researchers concluded that most of us worry unnecessarily. They also concluded that the majority of people live with a negative mindset most of their lives.

MOTOR VEHICLES ARE ENGINEERED TO MOVE FORWARD

If you think of a motor vehicle, its makers have designed it to move forward at different speed levels. Most light vehicles today have five forward gears and one reverse gear. The reverse gear is only used for the purpose of positioning the vehicle so that it moves forward in the right direction. Essentially, vehicles are engineered to move forward at different speed levels.

This is a good picture of man. We are so positively engineered. We possess the potential to succeed at anything we desire to achieve. As with vehicles, we are engineered to move in the five forward gears but the majority of us quickly shift into reverse gear most of the time. We are so negative about ourselves and our prospects. We view life with a negative mindset most of the time. For example, when we are faced with challenges, we wallow around our comfort zones or give up too easily. When we face setbacks, we give excuses why we should not press on, or we tend to look for people to blame.

No wonder we struggle to move forward in life. We attempt to move forward, but our minds are in reverse gear. Our faces and eyes may be looking forward, but our minds are looking backwards. So we actually remain stationary or move backward more than we go forward, because, usually what we do and where we go is determined largely by where we are looking and what we see in our minds' eyes.

POTENTIAL IS ABOUT WHAT WE CAN BE, NOT WHAT WE ARE

In Judges Chapter 6 the Bible tells the story of Gideon, a scared young man in Israel during the time the nation was under the dominion of the Midianites. While he was threshing wheat at a winepress, in fear and hidden from his enemies, an angel of God met him and said to him, *"God is with you, you mighty man of valour."* Gideon asked him, *"If God is with us, why has He allowed the Midianties to subdue and oppress us?"* The angel told him, *"Go in that strength of yours and save Israel. Am I not sending you?"*

But you know what Gideon did? He began to give excuses. He reminded God that his family was the poorest in the tribe of Manasseh, and he himself was the least in his family. He began to focus on his background and weaknesses, and the more he did, the more he convinced himself that he did not have what it took to be a leader.

You will note that while Gideon focused on who he was and his background, God spoke from the angle of the potential Gideon had to be a leader and a deliverer. In other words, while Gideon saw himself *as he was*, God saw what Gideon *could become*.

Gideon focused on his current station, while God spoke from the perspective of potential. You know what eventually happened. Gideon did end up delivering Israel from the hands of the enemy after God convinced him with a few miraculous signs.

While preaching on the subject of potential, I made the following statement:

> All that we know is not all that we *can* know.
> All that we have done is not all that we *can* do.
> All that we are is not all we *can* be. And all that we have is not all that we *can* have.

Do you think this is a true statement? I believe it is. We live way below our potential. We don't think hard enough. We don't really persist against difficulties and setbacks. We could be better people, do greater things, and have better lives, only if we believed so and did the things that would enable us to be better people, do greater things and have better lives.

THE NEED FOR SURVIVAL EXPOSES CREATIVE ABILITY

People who do not have regular income or are pressed to the corner with needs become creative. If you look closely at how people in squatter settlements conduct themselves, you will notice that they do the best with what they have. Nothing is useless. What well-to-do people throw away as useless is useful to the not-so-well-to-do. Their eyes and minds are more open because they do not know when their next meal is coming from. *They can turn a piece of trash into treasure.*

We used to accommodate a family from West Papua. The man had been a freedom fighter and had fled into Papua New Guinea from Indonesian soldiers. I noticed that although he was not highly educated, he was creative with a lot of things. For instance, he and his wife made beautiful flowers with different coloured strings. The guy could fix stereos, TV sets, microwaves, stoves, sewing machines, Coleman lamps, etc. He could play several musical instruments and sing beautifully. He even recorded an album while he stayed with us. I would go along with him to the studio and fetch water for him while he recorded his songs. He could build nice tables and beds, and the wife prepared delicious meals. They were very creative with what I and my wife considered to be trash.

One day I asked the man how come he was multi-talented. He told me that he had acquired much of the skills in the refugee camp at Wutung. He told me that in these camps most of the comforts of modern living were absent, so the people were forced to improvise with what they had. They were forced to become creative in order to make their lives as comfortable as possible.

For over fifteen years the Papua New Guinea government fought with the Bougainville Revolutionary Army. All businesses on the island closed and government services came to a standstill. People resorted to living the way their ancestors had lived. Because they could not make gardens due to fear of both the government soldiers and the rebels, they lived in the bush on what they could find. Many died from sicknesses and diseases, but many also survived. Many became creative. It has been reported that many people produced diesel from coconut oil to run their vehicles and generator sets and did a lot of creative things to ensure their survival.

My point in relating all these examples is this: When you do not have a job and are faced with the pressures of life, I believe that the chances of you becoming creative and innovative are greater.

EMPLOYEES COMPLY WITH STANDARD OPERATING PROCEDURES

Most employees are not allowed to use their imaginations and creativity. Instead, they are expected and even compelled to follow established ways of doing things, technically referred to as *standard operating procedures*. These procedures were set in place by people who developed the systems.

Employees are so engrossed in following standard procedures that they do not think even about making improvements to those procedures. In any case, why should they? Whether they find ways to improve the ways of doing things or not, they still get paid. There is really no incentive to think innovatively, because the pay comes as long as they consistently follow the procedures.

The worse thing is that junior employees who intentionally or inadvertently improvise and take short-cuts to the established systems and achieve results get penalized by their superiors, who are usually employees themselves. These people are penalized not because they have not achieved the desired results doing things differently, but because they have not complied with standard procedures. So the system creates fear for creativity and reinforces the forces that work against innovation.

Some employees who have seen different ways of doing things but have not been allowed the freedom to do so by the established systems have resigned and ventured out on their own. They have competed with their former employers by introducing improvements, and have usually succeeded. In fact that is another good thing about getting a job. You can learn about the business you are employed in, with a view to starting your own in future.

Let me encourage you with this: You have a greater chance of realizing your potential when you work for yourself than when you work for others. I know this from my own experience. I also know this from reading biographies and autobiographies of many financially successful people from different parts of the world.

REASON # 15

DEVELOP YOUR "SURVIVOR'S INSTINCT"

THERE IS A FIGHTING SPIRIT IN ALL OF US

WHAT WE NEED to realize is that there is a fighting spirit in all of us. That spirit lays dormant most of our lives, and awakens only to challenges and threats. The need for survival brings that spirit to the fore.

In *Life After Graduation* I tell the story of the man who scaled a high wall when chased by a huge dog. The fear of being torn into pieces by the dog awakened the "survivor's instinct" in him that he was able to scale the wall. When he tried to do the same under normal circumstances, he found that he could not.

It is said that during the 1906 earthquake and fire in San Francisco, invalids actually got up and fled for their lives. These people had lain helpless in bed for many years but the fear of getting burned plus the desire to live caused their limbs to straighten and strengthen such that they could get out of bed and run away from the blazing fires.

I recall an incident where we chased a wild cow. It had

been pursued by a neighboring clan and we had taken on the chase when it entered our territory. The animal must have run a long distance, and we could see its legs becoming wobbly as it ran through our village.

Some of us thought we were very close to catching it when it seemingly ran out of breath and strength. Suddenly it stopped running, turned around and began stomping towards us with fury in its eyes. All of us expected the animal to continue running, and none of us expected it to start chasing us! The moment we saw anger in its eyes and its nose puffing spit and turning red, we knew we were in danger. All of us fled for our lives, and the cow just strode back with ease.

I learnt a valuable lesson that day. It is that when you are pursued, turn around and fight back instead of taking on your heels and running. Your enemies, who may take all kinds of forms, could be pursuing you *because you are running*. They like looking at the back of your head and heels when you take flight. The moment you stop and stare at them in the face, they will melt, because they can sense the fighting spirit rising in you. You will be fighting for survival, whereas they have been pursuing you because that was easy for them to do with you running from them.

THE SURVIVOR'S INSTINCT IN MAN IS MULTI-FACETED

If you chase a pig or a dog into a corner, the survivor's instinct in it will awaken, and it will strike back. The same survivor's instinct resides in human beings. But unlike animals, whose instinct is either to fight or flee, the survivor's instinct in man is multi-faceted, creative and innovative. Sometimes it attacks, which is a manifestation of the crude part of that instinct. At other times it finds more creative ways of dealing with threats and challenges.

The human mind has the ability to develop new ways of handling threats and needs within a very short time–in fact on the spur of the moment or in an instant if need necessitates it.

PAID JOBS MAKE PEOPLE MENTALLY LAZY

Entrepreneurs and those who venture out and take risks see this potential come to the fore more often than those who wallow around the comforts of paid jobs. In fact, jobs make people comfortable and complacent, and to a great extent lazy, when it comes to using their minds.

CREATIVE THINKING IS THE HARDEST OF JOBS

Scientists say that the average person uses up only 10% of their brain capacity all of their lives. The remaining 90% is unused until the person dies and goes into the grave. It becomes food for maggots and worms. We do not use our mind to its full potential.

If you think about all the inventions of man since the dawn of creation, it has all been the product of the mind. What was invented actually existed in the inventors' minds before the items became tangible. God did not create the aeroplane, for instance. When He breathed into the nostrils of Adam, He imparted something of His creative ability into man. He gave man the ability to discover the principles of flight and perfect it over time until he was able to fly faster, higher and longer than the birds of the air.

The mind of man has much greater potential than man has been able to utilize in his lifetime. It has the potential to think up solutions to the most pressing problems facing mankind. Its ability to accommodate, assimilate, and process information inputted into it by the five senses has yet to be matched by the most advanced computers in the world.

A THINKER, AN ASSET

I once read an interesting story. It was about this expert who was engaged by a company that was facing problems–one of those so-called "corporate doctors." He was asked to review the entire organisation and recommend measures which in his expert opinion would, if applied, see the company experience a turnaround in sales and profitability. So the expert went to work. He spent several weeks in the office going through all the systems, positions and people that made up the organisation.

The story goes that every time he went up to the top floor where the owners usually had their offices, he would notice this fellow in the office facing the boss's office laying back in his chair with his feet up on the table top. Sometimes he was absent for days. The expert wondered who this person could be. When he checked the payroll files, he was very surprised to learn that this person was the highest paid in the organisation. The expert noticed that this fellow earned even more than the owners.

When the expert finally presented his report to the directors, he recommended that the company should be downsized, a good number of positions and their functions should be merged or chopped, and the people who occupied those positions should be laid off.

At the top of the list of people recommended for dismissal was this fellow in the top floor office. The expert's reasoning was that he had seen this gentleman napping at work all the time he had been reviewing the company's systems and procedures. He was really a liability to the company, seeing he was the highest paid.

It was when he was presenting his report that he truly learnt about this seemingly unproductive gentleman's work. The owners told the expert that his recommendation for the gentleman to be relieved of his services would take the company down rather than help it to rise, because the guy he had seen "napping" was actually the person who had developed the ideas for the products the company had come to be known for. One of the directors told the expert, *"He is the brains behind the company. We pay him to think!"*

Imagine the shock the expert received! He had made the biggest blunder of his professional life when he recommended the sacking of the person whom the company owners considered their biggest asset, because he was a thinker. He went to the office and sat in his chair, or went to some quiet place, and used his imagination to think up products the company could design and sell to the consuming public. The fact that the company paid him highly is an indication of the success they experienced when they took his advice.

Many organisations now have "think tanks." These are

groups of people who meet to talk about solutions to problems. They are a group of people who are considered to be thinkers. They are highly paid, and their advice is highly sought out. Some "think tanks" are private organisations which are established to conduct research into problems and develop solutions, which they sell to governments and companies for large amounts.

EVERYONE CAN THINK BUT ONLY A FEW THINK CREATIVELY

Everyone can think, but not many engage in *active* and *creative* thinking. That is why "consulting" and coaching are the fastest-growing industries worldwide. Most people are too busy with life's issues that they leave research, analysis and serious thinking to consultants, who charge hefty prices for their advice, which are the product of their minds.

In fact it has been said that the hottest products on the market today are "info-products" or information products. In the Information Age, there is an unquenchable thirst for new knowledge and information. Everything happens so fast that those with the latest information are able to outdo the competition. That is why at one stage CNN's motto was "*Be the first to know.*" Researchers, analysts and thinkers are tapping into this info-products market and are becoming very rich without too much sweat.

I believe that most people who work for a regular salary do not really think. They do think, but what I mean is, they do not engage in the kind of thinking that is *creative, lateral, outside-the-box*. The regularity in the salary provided by the employer is a major factor that induces this mental laziness. They are not pressed to think, because, once again, whether they think hard or not, they still get paid.

In comparison, entrepreneurs and self-employed people tend to think more actively as well as deeply. Their thinking has *width* and *depth*. They allow their imaginations to devise ways out of their situations. They do not have money coming in regularly, so they are forced to think hard. And they do come up with creative solutions which serve a lot of people, thereby making them richer but also taking the rest of society forward.

I am convinced that self-employment brings out the hidden potential in a person. It engenders creativity. It creates an environment that is conducive for the imaginative and creative ability of man to come alive. It helps people to think hard and deep. It awakens and develops their "survivor' instinct."

If you want to know what you are really made of, consider getting into business. You will become aware of strengths and abilities you did not know you possessed until you do so. Your "survivor's instinct" will emerge more often and readily than when you work for others.

REASON # 16

PROTECT YOUR ASSETS

WHEN YOU WORK for a fortnightly salary, you hold all your possessions in your name. If you own a house or a car, it is your personal asset. If anything happens to you, it affects what you own, and if anything happens to your possessions, you feel the pinch personally. You and what you own are one. If you owe debts which you cannot pay, the debtors can lay hold of what you own. Or if your vehicle runs over someone, you will pay compensation out of your own account.

A BUSINESS IS A "CORPORATE PERSON"

If you are self-employed and operate under a corporate entity such as a company, you can protect your money and other assets by keeping them under the company's name instead of your own.

This is because under the law, a company becomes a separate legal entity. You create a 'corporate person' when you register a company. This corporate person has certain legal rights enjoyed by a human person. For instance, a company can sue people or other companies, and be sued itself. So if you operate under a company and shelter your assets under it, people who sue you personally will never touch your company's assets. That is how rich people protect their assets.

This is a very important reason to be in business, because today's world is very litigious. That is to say, people are more willing to sue others and claim large amounts for small misdemeanors. In the United States, for instance, it is said that lawsuits are being filed at a rate of one hundred million a year. These cases have nothing to do with right and wrong. They are basically predicated on the desire of some parties to extract wealth from others.

'Compensation' has become a very commonly-used word in Papua New Guinea, which has developed a culture of its own. In such a setting, it is vital that you shelter or protect your personal assets rather than leave them vulnerable to other people making a claim on them for whatever reason. For example, if you invest in real estate or buy shares through a company, not many people will know what you do and own.

THE LIABILITY OF COMPANY OWNERS IS LIMITED

Another point is the concept of "limited liability" which certain companies enjoy. If you see the words "limited" or "Ltd" after an organisation's name, it is a limited liability company.

What this means is that the liabilities or obligations of the business owners is limited to the investment they have made in establishing the company. In the event the company cannot meet its commitments to the bank or other creditors, or the company is wound up, creditors cannot touch the business owners. They can only get paid from what the company has in its name.

If the company does not have anything or much of value which the creditors can sell and recoup their money, they have to treat what is owed as bad debts. They can force the company to bankruptcy but cannot touch the owners. The owners can always start another company after the first one has gone into bankruptcy.

This fact has become clear in a long-standing legal battle between two companies. One company had advanced another company a significant amount of money which the borrower refused to repay, saying that the lender had prevented it from carrying on business, as the lender was the regulator of the industry the borrower operated in. The case was protracted and expensive, taking over ten years to bring to conclusion.

When it finally came to an end, the courts decided that the borrower indeed owed the lender the money, which was computed to be principal plus interest over ten years. The amount turned out to be over K100 million.

However, when the lender tried to effect the court's decision, it was shocked to find that the borrower was operating under a different company from the one which had borrowed the money in the first place. The debtor asked the court to make the company principal personally responsible for his company's debts, but this was not possible. He had cleverly entered into an agreement and borrowed the money using one company, then changed the company name and transferred all his assets to the new company while the court case was in progress.

The old company did not have any assets which the creditor company could take possession of, even after the court decided in its favour. The principal himself could not be held responsible either. Even if the court decided that he should pay up, he would be declared bankrupt, because he does not own anything in his own name.

The important point to note in this case is that the principal of the company who borrowed the money could not be personally held responsible for what his company owed. This is because the law gives recognition to his company as being completely separate and different from him as a person.

This is what I mean when I say that you can protect your assets when you work for yourself under a corporate entity. There is no such protection for those who work for others and own assets in their own names.

LITTLE ASSET PROTECTION FOR SOLE TRADERS AND PARTNERSHIPS

What I have discussed above only applies to those who operate under companies. If you work for yourself as a sole trader, or in partnership with someone else, you cannot protect your assets as you can do under a company.

A sole trader operates in his own name. His assets are in his name. His liability is unlimited. If his business folds, he will be personally liable for the debts owed by the business.

A partnership is a group of two or more people who have come together to carry out business. They may operate under a business name but they are individually responsible for the business's liabilities.

Both sole traders and partnerships do not enjoy the tax advantages discussed in Chapter 18. They are charged tax at the personal income rate, which is higher than the rate applied to companies.

NO ASSET PROTECTION FOR EMPLOYEES

I have discussed the ability of companies, partnerships and sole traders to protect their assets, to make this point: *Employees cannot protect their assets.* What they own is vulnerable to litigation and extortion, because they own everything in their own name.

If you work for yourself, my encouragement is for you to operate under a company so that you can be able to keep your assets under the company's name instead of your own.

REASON # 17

ENJOY TAX ADVANTAGES AVAILABLE TO THE INFORMAL SECTOR

THERE ARE ECONOMIC activities which you can carry out for yourself which the government does not require you to register with or report to anyone. In other words, you can become self-employed in the informal sector.

This sector is so large and worth hundreds of millions in Papua New Guinea, that the government has passed a law called the *Informal Sector Development And Control Act 2004* which recognizes the importance of informal businesses and provides some guidelines and regulations on how it should operate. This is another reason you should seriously consider becoming self-employed.

What the law requires is that people in the informal sector abide by sanitary and other laws. They are not required to lodge returns to authorities on how much they earn, or to pay taxes like employees or companies. What they earn is 100% theirs.

In my view, the Act provides the best opportunity for the

thousands of unemployed people in Papua New Guinea to become meaningfully engaged in the economic development of the country. The sector has the capacity to accommodate the thousands of school leavers that are being produced by the education system. It provides the best option for those who out of frustration and hopelessness have turned to crime, to earn an honest living and contribute as productive members of society.

THE HIGHER YOU RISE UP THE LADDER, THE MORE TAX YOU PAY

When you are employed by someone else, you pay more in income tax. The harder you work and the higher you rise up the corporate ladder, the more you earn; and the more you earn, the higher you rise in the tax bracket, and therefore the more you are taxed.

Every time you get a pay rise through promotion and move from one tax bracket to the next, or even receive an adjustment to keep up with the general level of prices (the Consumer Price Index or CPI), the Government gets a raise as well.

Let us look at some actual figures. According to the 2019 Income Tax Schedule effective from 1st January 2019, the following tax rates applied for people who had no dependents and had lodged their tax declarations:

- Where fortnightly income exceeds K950, tax is calculated as K115.38 plus 30 toea for every kina by which income exceeds K950.

- Where fortnightly income exceeds K1,276, tax is calculated as K213.46 plus 35 toea for every kina by which income exceeds K1,276.

- Where fortnightly income exceeds K2,700, tax is calculated as K711.54 plus 40 toea for every kina by which income exceeds K2,700.

- Where fortnightly income exceeds K9,623, tax is calculated as K3,480.77 plus 42 toea for every kina by which income exceeds K9,623.

Tax paid by someone earning K950 in a fortnight would be K115. This would work out to 12% of gross income. The person who earns K9,623 would pay K3,481 per fortnight.

How about someone who earns K1,000 in a fortnight? He would pay K50 [i.e. K1,000 − K950] x 0.30 = K15 + K115 = K130. His net take-home pay would be K870. In fact it would be lower because the employer would have to deduct the employee's superannuation contribution which currently stands at 6% of gross income or K60. So the actual net income the person receives into his account would be K810.

How much tax would someone earning K6,000 in a fortnight pay? It would be K3,300 (i.e. K6,000 − K2,700) x 0.40 = K1,320 + K712 = K2,032. His take-home pay, including superannuation, would be only K3,608 [i.e. K6,000 − K2,032 (tax) − K360 (superannuation)].

Note that income is defined as *"salary, wages, commission, bonus, remuneration of any kind, whether at piece work rate or otherwise, in respect of or in relation to the employment of that person as an employee.*" Benefits such as motor vehicles and housing are taken as part of the employee's remuneration and taxed in full. If such benefits are paid to an employee in cash, the amounts are added to the salary for tax purposes.

If these benefits are provided by the employer, the Tax Office has prescribed rates to be applied for tax purposes. For instance, if an employee is provided a high cost house or flat (defined as *"any unit of accommodation which would fetch more than K800,000 if sold on the open market, and in any other case for which the market rental is more than K3,000 per week"*), the prescribed rate to be added to the fortnightly salary is K700 per fortnight for Area 1 centres (Goroka, Lae, Madang, Mount Hagen and Port Moresby). For a vehicle supplied with fuel, the prescribed rate for tax purposes is K125 per fortnight

EMPLOYEES WORK MORE FOR THEIR EMPLOYERS AND THE GOVERNMENT THAN FOR THEMSELVES

Basically what this means is that people who work hard for their employers receive pay rises and improved benefits which places them at higher tax brackets, with the result that they pay more and more tax. The gross figures may look enticing but what they actually take home is not that impressive. They effectively work for the Government without realizing it.

For example, someone earning K6,000 per fortnight (K156,000 per year) would be working more than four months or one third of the year just to pay income tax to the government, and eight months for themselves. A CEO earning K500,000 per year (K19,231 per fortnight) in salaries and other taxable benefits would be paying K195,422 in tax per annum. This would amount to working a little under five months of the year for the government and seven for themselves.

Paying higher taxes is not necessarily a bad thing. As responsible citizens, we all need to contribute towards meeting the costs of developing our country. When we work, either for ourselves or for others, we contribute to nation-building. When we pay taxes, we empower the government to employ public servants to provide us services, build good roads, schools and hospitals, make laws and ensure that everyone complies with those laws so that we can all live in peace.

But did you know that not everyone pays tax? Did you know that the law allows some people to legally minimise their taxes or even not pay tax at all even though they make more? Did you know that some people are given "tax holidays" by the government? Did you know that the already rich and well-to-do are given "tax breaks," "tax concessions," "tax rebates," and "tax credits" which are not available to employees?

The personal income tax system is based on the PAYE principle, which is "pay-as-you-earn." What this means is that you are taxed on your gross income, *before* you make any deductions for the costs you have incurred in earning that income. Such costs might include rent for the house you are living in (if not rented by your employer and you are not entitled to housing allowance), or fuel and maintenance of the vehicle which you drive to and from work, the food you eat in order to stay alive and keep on working, the clothes you wear, the power and telephone bill for your house, gas, bus fares, etc.

Under the PAYE system, you are required to pay your income tax as you earn your fortnightly or monthly income, before you meet your living and other personal expenses. And to make it easy for you as well as to ensure that you do pay up, the government has directed your employers to deduct the tax the moment you get paid.

So basically what happens is that the government gets its tax income from your salary *before* you see your pay cheque. The employer issues you a pay slip showing how much your gross income has been, and the deductions such as tax and superannuation. You can apply for tax rebates for expenses such as school fees, but it takes time, and there is no guarantee that you will receive a rebate from the Internal Revenue Commission. In fact rebates for school fees no longer apply from 2019 onwards.

Let me admit that I am not a professional tax advisor. You need to find out more from a qualified tax consultant or accountant, but the point is that when you work for others, you end up paying more in income tax. You effectively work for the government for between a quarter and half of the year, and the rest for yourself.

If you take into account the 10% Goods and Services Tax (GST) you pay every time you purchase goods and services, and the 15% Interest Withholding Tax you pay on interest you earn from your savings with the bank, the government probably ends up with 50% of your income.

THE SELF-EMPLOYED WORK 100% FOR THEMSELVES AND PAY LESS TAX

When you become self-employed, you work for yourself 100% of the time.

If the business activity you are engaged in is considered an informal activity, you are not required to get registered with the Investment Promotion Authority or the Tax Office. This means your gross income becomes your net income. In other words, you keep all the income you earn. You are not required to report how much you earn to anybody. For example, if you are into farming for a living or operate a Public Motor Vehicle, the government does not require you to report or pay taxes on what you earn. It is all yours to keep and spend and invest as you wish. That is the beauty of being self-employed.

Have you noticed that small business people or those who are self-employed seem to have more money in their pockets and bank accounts compared with those who work for salaries and wages? How come uneducated self-employed people can buy land and build their own houses whereas those working for companies and the government cannot afford to?

How come self-employed people can travel around in good vehicles while well-educated employees own run-down and unroadworthy vehicles or catch public transport all their lives?

How come many self-employed people travel overseas regularly while people who have jobs cannot even pay for holidays in other parts of the country?

How come most employed people borrow a lot from self-employed people?

Income tax is one major reason. The self-employed pay little or no income tax, while the employed get hit with tax which can amount to large amounts of money. In fact, when you think about it, income tax is probably the largest single expense paid by those who work for others.

Employed people work more for their employers, the government, their debtors, the suppliers of good and services, and less for themselves. They work for other people such that what they actually have left with them at the end of two weeks is very little if anything. So they go back to work again, because if they miss just one fortnight, they would be technically bankrupt.

FOR THE EMPLOYED, PAY FRIDAY IS PAYDAY; FOR THE SELF-EMPLOYED, ANY DAY IS PAYDAY!

In Papua New Guinea you can tell when it is government or company payday. You see long queues at the banks and shopping centres especially on pay Wednesdays or Fridays. You can sense life and vitality in people. You also see a lot of relatives of working people in town that have come for their share. The way towns are flooded on paydays, you will think that everyone works and has come into town to get paid.

If you ask a self-employed person whether a certain Friday is government or company payday, he will scratch his head and say he does not know. Do you think he is lying? No! He is telling the truth, because he does not follow these days. It is not part of his mental framework. For him, any day is payday! Let me repeat that: *For the self-employed, any day is payday.* He either makes something, or he doesn't. When he has money, he goes shopping. When he doesn't, he is busy working.

His income is irregular. Sometimes he makes nothing; other times he makes a lot. His lifestyle seems risky to someone who is used to living on regular fortnightly pay. But that is the way the self-employed live. I can tell you from experience that it is more exciting and rewarding than the monotonous, and I should add boring kind of life which employed people live: Going through the same daily routine for years.

REASON # 18

ENJOY TAX ADVANTAGES AVAILABLE TO COMPANIES

THERE ARE MANY tax advantages available to people who are in business for themselves, which are unavailable to employees. This chapter covers those who register their businesses with the Investment Promotion Authority and the Internal Revenue Commission as companies.

TAX ADVANTAGES FOR COMPANIES

If you operate under a company, there are many tax advantages available to business owners which are not available to those who work for salaries. Here are eight of the major advantages.

TAX ADVANTAGE # 1
LOWER TAX RATE

Company tax rates are lower than personal income tax rates. Companies resident in the country (i.e. those that are incorporated in the country or have the majority of managers and shareholders living in the country) pay a flat 30% tax on profits (for non-resident companies the rate is 48%).

When business people succeed, they create jobs which benefit many other people. When employees succeed, they get pay rises which benefit only themselves and their immediately families. That is why the government either does not tax businesses at all, or taxes them at a lower rate than the rates it applies for employees.

The government uses the tax laws to reward those who take risks and provide jobs. Sometimes the government even pays businesses to invest and create jobs.

TAX ADVANTAGE # 2
TAX PAID AT END OF YEAR

Employees are taxed fortnightly or monthly, depending on when they are paid by their employers. They pay as they earn. As mentioned above, they do not even see the tax component of their income. What they do see is only a figure on the pay slip.

Companies on the other hand pay tax at the end of each year. They can use the cash they generate for the whole year to meet expenses and make more before they pay tax, whereas employees do not have access to the tax-equivalent of the cash they earn.

Note that sometimes the Tax Office may require businesses to make interim company tax payments either quarterly or half-yearly. In this way the government gets access to tax income in advance of profits being declared. If it is found at the end of the reporting period that companies have paid more than they should have, the balance is refunded to them. Normally, the interim payments would be deducted from what the company is supposed to pay, and the company pays the balance at the end of the reporting period when it submits its tax returns.

What effectively happens is that companies pay tax at the end of the year whereas employees pay throughout the year as they earn.

TAX ADVANTAGE # 3
TAX PAID ON PROFITS, NOT INCOME

Companies pay tax on their *profits*, while employees pay tax on their *gross income*. Companies deduct all their business (or operating) expenses first and pay tax on what is left (if there is anything at all), while employees pay tax first and meet their living expenses with after-tax income.

The timing of tax payment for companies and employees is as follows:

Companies	Employees
1. Earn	1. Earn
2. Spend	2. Pay tax
3. Pay tax	3. Spend

Companies earn, spend, and pay tax (if at all), while employees earn, pay tax and spend (always). Companies spend gross (before-tax) income while employees spend net (after-tax) income. The words *if at all* are added above because in some circumstances companies may make profit but they don't pay any tax. This will become clear as you read the rest of this chapter.

TAX ADVANTAGE # 4
ALLOWABLE DEDUCTIONS

Under the tax laws, all expenses incurred by a company in earning its income are referred to as 'allowable deductions.' This means that the Tax Office allows companies to deduct these expenses from the company's gross annual revenue. Tax is applied on whatever is left as 'profit,' which is defined as income less expenses.

There are no such 'allowable deductions' for employees. For instance, if an employee uses his own vehicle to go to work, the expenses involved in owning and maintaining the vehicle are not 'allowable deductions' under the Tax Act, even though he uses the vehicle to go to work and earn income on which he pays tax. On the other hand a company's vehicle operating costs are allowed to be deducted from income before taxes are paid.

If an employee is provided a vehicle by his employer, he pays tax on the use of the vehicle. Or if he receives a vehicle allowance for the use of his own vehicle, he still pays tax on that allowance.

TAX ADVANTAGE # 5
DEPRECIATION

Companies are also allowed to *depreciate* their capital items such as property, vehicles, office equipment, furniture, etc. Depreciation represents the decline in the value of a capital item due to its use. What companies do is to calculate the depreciation component each year using depreciation schedules issued by the Tax Office, apply the appropriate rates, and deduct the amount from the company's gross income in the year.

For instance, assume that a company purchases a vehicle for K200,000. For depreciation purposes, the Tax Office might stipulate that depreciation be charged at 30% every year. In this case, the company would deduct K60,000 from the vehicle's book value and add this amount to its operating expenses in the first year. The new book value of the vehicle will be K140,000. In the second year, the depreciation to be deducted and added to expenses would be 30% of K140,000 which is K42,000. This amount would be added to the second year's expenses and the book value will fall to K98,000. The process will go on until the book value is reduced to zero.

Sometimes the Tax Office allows companies to determine the useful lifespan of the vehicle and deduct the value in equal amounts every year. For instance, if the lifetime of the K200,000 vehicle is 5 years, depreciation will be charged at K40,000 every year.

In this way the government allows companies to recoup what they spent to purchase on capital items, as well as to save for their replacement. What effectively happens is that the government indirectly pays for the replacement of these items by making depreciation an 'allowable deduction.' Depreciation is one way companies significantly reduce their taxable income, especially after they have purchased large capital items. And it is one of the main reasons why some companies can make a lot in profits but pay little or no tax—by adding the depreciation deductions to expenses and massively reducing taxable income.

Let us look at an example. Say a company records a net

income of K100,000 after deducting all its operating expenses minus depreciation. If depreciation on its machinery and other capital items such as vehicles and buildings is K200,000, the company will report that it has made a *loss* of K100,000. This is not actually a loss in terms of cash. It is merely a book or paper loss allowed to be deducted under the tax laws. Some people refer to this as a "phantom loss."

So because the company did not make a profit, it will not pay any tax. The amount it would have paid in tax without provision for depreciation is held back by the company and reinvested into the business. In this way the 'phantom loss' becomes actual cash which can be invested.

An employee who owns a house or vehicle is not allowed to make deductions from their income to account for the decline in the value of the assets held in their own name. They can only maintain and replace those assets with their net or after-tax income. When their income is reduced or removed for any reason, the asset can easily become a liability in terms of the costs associated with owning and maintaining it.

Likewise, an employee who is paying interest on a loan he has taken to purchase a vehicle or house cannot claim the interest component while a company can do so as a cost of financing the business.

TAX ADVANTAGE # 6
LOSS CARRY FORWARD PROVISIONS

Another advantage of operating as a self-employed person under a company is that the government allows companies to carry forward accounting losses for 7 years. What this means is that if a company makes a loss in the first year of operations, it can deduct that loss against the following 6 years' profits. Essentially, if a company suffers losses, it can write those losses off against profits in subsequent years over the next 7 years.

An example will clarify this. Say a company incurs a loss of K10,000 in Year 1 and makes a profit of K15,000 in Year 2. It will pay tax on only K5,000 in Year 2. The K10,000 profit in Year 2 will be used to offset the K10,000 loss in Year 1, and tax will apply on the balance of profit in Year 2 which is K5,000. If the company makes a loss in Year 2 as well, this amount will be added to the first year's loss and the total amount is carried forward to the third year, and so on.

If a company makes a loss of K10,000 in Year 1, a loss again of K15,000 in Year 2, and a profit of K30,000 in Year 3, it will write off K25,000 against the previous years' losses and pay tax on only K5,000 in Year 3. If the profit in Year 3 is K20,000, it will report a loss of K5,000 for tax purposes, and carry that amount forward to Year 4. If in Year 4 it makes a profit of K10,000, it will pay tax on K5,000 only.

TAX ADVANTAGE # 7
REFUNDS FOR GST

Companies which are registered with the Tax Office for Goods & Services Tax (GST, previously value-added tax or VAT) receive refunds for the GST they pay for the goods and services they buy in the course of conducting their businesses. Currently the GST is 10% of the transaction price. The Tax Office requires that companies whose annual turnover exceeds K250,000 register for GST while those generating less than K250,000 can register on a voluntary basis. Businesses that are not registered cannot charge GST on their customers.

A GST-registered company that purchases goods and services from GST-registered suppliers receives an input credit of 10% of the total cost of inputs. When it sells goods and services, it is required to collect and remit 10% of the sales to the Tax Office at the end of the month.

What actually happens is that the company deducts the GST it has collected from its buyers from the GST it has paid to its suppliers in a particular month. The balance is remitted to the Tax Office with a return showing the collections and pay outs. If the GST it has paid to its suppliers exceeds what it has collected from its buyers in that month, the Tax Office refunds the difference.

Individual people such as employees pay GST in full every time they purchase goods and services from GST- registered suppliers, but they do not get any refunds. This also includes informal sector operators, sole traders and companies whose annual turnover is less than K250,000, unless they have voluntarily registered for GST.

TAX ADVANTAGE # 8
SOME PERSONAL EXPENSES CAN BE TRANSFERRED TO THE COMPANY

A further tax advantage is that certain personal-related expenses can be treated as business expenses, and hence be claimed against company profits. Such expenses can include rent and electricity (if you work from home), vehicle expenses, medical expenses, school fees, travel, etc, if you write these benefits into your contract of employment with your own company.

Let me warn you however that you need to seek expert advice from an accountant or tax advisor on this as you may be charged for *tax evasion* if you do not know what you are doing.

Under the law, *tax avoidance*, which involves arranging your business in a way that minimizes or even avoids tax altogether, is legal. The tax legislation provides many loopholes for tax avoidance. The different tax advantages discussed in this chapter are examples of loopholes allowed by the law for people to legally minimize or avoid tax.

Tax evasion on the other hand, which is manipulating the accounting books so as to escape paying taxes, is illegal.

You need to obtain professional advice to ensure that you are avoiding taxes and not evading them.

You can see that there are many tax advantages which a company has available to its owner, while those who work for fortnightly salaries and wage do not enjoy any advantages at all. In fact, they are hard-hit by taxes. They work hard to make their employers rich, and they work for the government.

I hope that you can see how the tax laws favour business owners and are against job holders. In fact, tax is one of the main factors which separates the rich from the poor and working class.

Aren't the tax advantages alone reason enough for you to seriously consider becoming your own boss by setting up a company and trading products or services rather than trading your time, energy, knowledge and skills—essentially your life—for a salary that is highly taxed?

CONCLUSION

ARE YOU CONVINCED?

I have related how I decided in 2001 to never work for a fortnightly salary again. When I made that decision, I did not know what I have related in this book. If I had not been forced to a corner as I was then, it is most probable that I would never have become self-employed. Getting sacked has been the most defining moment in my life. It has changed the course of our lives as a family.

The Bible says that the Word of God is sharper than a two-edged sword. A double-edged sword can cut both forward and backwards. So preaching the Word of God can challenge and transform both the hearers and the preacher.

In the same vein, I can testify that writing this book has really changed me. I do not know about you, but I have become challenged in the process of writing this book. I am convinced that if I were working for someone today, or looking for a job, I would get into business for myself sooner rather than later. But seeing that I am already self-employed, this book has validated the decision I made in 2001 never to work for a salary again. I am therefore going to go for it. I have eighteen reasons to do so. The question is: *"How about you?"*

A CHANGE IN THINKING MAY BE NECESSARY

Everything that we say and do is an outward manifestation of the inward thoughts that we think. In other words, our thoughts are the seeds we sow, which, when they sprout over time, produce the plants of our words, actions, attitudes. The ultimate fruits of our thoughts are the kinds of people we become and the lives we live.

If you really analyse your life, the kind of person you are now is a reflection of those ideas. Those ideas and thoughts have been so strong as to influence the decisions and choices you have made in your life up to now.

This is what Emerson observed regarding the relationship between our thoughts, actions, habits and where we end up in life:

> Sow a thought, reap an action
> Sow an action, reap a habit
> Sow a habit, reap a character
> Sow a character, reap a destiny.

What Emerson observed is actually what the Bible has proclaimed for centuries: *"Be careful how you think, because your life is shaped by your thoughts."*

Some functions of our bodies are involuntary, meaning that we do not think and act in order for the different parts of our bodies to respond and work. For instance, our hearts pump without us thinking and doing anything about it. Our lungs inhale oxygen and exhale carbon dioxide without us deciding that we will breathe. We also have no control over how our nervous or digestive systems work. They function automatically.

But many other actions are voluntary, and they originate in our minds as thoughts. Our actions are our thoughts in motion. Or as it is said, *"Thought is ancestor to deed."* And our words are verbalised thoughts, meaning what we say with our tongues and lips is actually our thoughts expressed as words coming from our lips.

I hope and trust that I have sown some seeds in your mind which will motivate and even compel you to seriously think about becoming your own boss. If one part of your mind likes the idea of becoming self-employed and being your own boss but another part resists the idea, you need to aggressively take control of your mind, bring those negative thoughts into captivity, and make your mind submit to the possibility of being self-employed.

It is said that the mind is the greatest battle field. Battles are won or lost in the mind before they become manifest outwardly. In most games, mental toughness is equally if not more important than physical preparation.

I once heard a preacher make this statement:

> If you win on the inside, you will win on the outside; if you lose on the inside, you will lose on the outside.

This is so true. If you are able to convince yourself in your mind that you can live a better life being self-employed, you will succeed; but if you fear imagining a life without a regular pay cheque, you will never venture out. You will become defeated in your mind. Fear will cripple and paralyse you to the extent that you do not take any action towards becoming your own boss.

A RENEWED MIND LEADS TO A TRANSFORMED LIFE

Let me quote a profound verse from the Bible. In his letter to the Roman Christians, the Apostle Paul made a life-changing statement when he wrote: *"Be ye not conformed to the world, but be ye transformed by the renewing of your mind. Then you will know the will of God—His good, acceptable and perfect will."*

Paul was writing about the word of God renewing peoples' minds as they heard and meditated on it. The Bible contains the thoughts of God. What Paul said is that as people think the positive and liberating thoughts of God, the negative and limiting thoughts of the world which they have grown up with will be neutralized; and the more they think as God thinks, their minds will be made new; the more new thoughts they think, the more they will experience transformation in life.

The Greek word for "transformed" is *metamorphoō*, from which we get the English word "metamorphosis." Metamorphosis refers to one thing changing into something completely different, for instance, a tadpole changing into a frog. The idea behind Paul's use of the word in the verse quoted above is actually a caterpillar changing into a butterfly. Can you imagine a caterpillar which crawls on a branch changing into a butterfly and souring the heights? That is the transformation

Paul said people would experience if they allowed the word of God to renew their minds.

Up to the time you started reading this book, you have been carrying many old ideas around–ideas you gathered from your parents, teachers, society, companions, etc. One of those ideas which the education system has programmed into your consciousness is that the only way you can live after graduating from school is by working for someone for a fortnightly salary.

Now you know that having a job is not the only way to live. You need to allow the information you have gathered from reading this book to transform your thinking so that you begin to accept another world–the world of self-employment, financial independence and financial freedom–than what school has programmed you into expecting: a world of minding other peoples' business for a pittance called a salary.

NOW THAT YOU HAVE TAKEN THE JOURNEY...

This book has been like taking a journey. After reading it, I know that some of your old ideas and mentalities have been challenged and shattered. It may also be that the very foundations of your mindsets have been shaken. For instance, your ideas about a paid job being the only way to live have been shaken, and new ideas about a life without a pay cheque and slavery to an employer have been introduced into your mind.

Albert Einstein has made this very profound statement:

> The mind that opens to a new idea never returns to its original size.

Think about that for a moment and you will agree that this has been the experience in your life already. By reading this book, your mind has been stretched and expanded and your way of thinking challenged.

If you look back on your life, whenever your mind has accommodated a new idea and you have believed in it, your life has been impacted by that idea. For instance, when you have come to accept and believe that God exists, it has been very hard for you to dislodge that belief from your mind. You may not live an upright life but every time you do something wrong, you feel guilty about it and become fearful, because you know that God has seen what you did.

Likewise, when you believe and accept the idea of becoming self-employed through your own business, you will never be the same again. You may be looking for a job or already have one, but you will not be satisfied until you become self-employed.

I hope that your mind has been expanded by the ideas contained in this book. I also hope that your mind will not go back to its original size with its old self-limiting ideas and imaginations. I hope that your mind has expanded enough for you to accommodate and accept a life without a regular pay cheque as a real possibility for you.

You now have a choice. You can either dismiss the new ideas you have acquired from this book and remain the same person you have been and live the same kind of life you have been living, or you can let these new ideas renew your mind and eventually lead you to a place where your life is transformed as you think seriously and take whatever action is necessary to see a change in your life and destiny.

Let me end our journey by quoting Michael J. Lowe again:

> Human beings charged with empowering beliefs can accomplish anything, including things others are certain are impossible.

I hope the reasons and ideas I have presented in this book have been empowering for you. And I hope that after taking the journey, becoming self-employed and minding your own business is now within your realm of possibility.

As I have mentioned, this book has impacted my own life. I have written it based on personal experience, and in the process the decision I made to become self-employed has become reinforced and cemented. I only wish that I had known what I have written, or read a book such as this one when I was a student or was just commencing work life. If I had, I would have left school with a different mindset. I am sure that I would have become a more prudent manager of my income over the first few years of working and therefore be financially better off today.

You are therefore in a much better position than I have been, now that you have read this book.

I encourage you to read this book over and over until it sinks into your heart and mind. Allow the words in this book to not only challenge you but also transform you. Feel free to underline, colour, or put stars around the points that stand out to you (assuming that the book is yours and not borrowed). You might also want to write those points on a different piece of paper. The actual act of rewriting will reinforce as well as clarify your understanding and aid your memory. Meditate on statements that challenge your mindset until the old, fearful ideas are neutralised and replaced by more empowering ones.

This is what I read in a magazine:

> If your book's cover is well-worn, it's corners dog-eared and its pages marked like a test you failed in high school, that's the surest sign that you not only got through the book, *but that the book got through you.*

I have many books in my library which I have bought and read through at least once, but there are some that I have read through several times, and a few I have studied from cover to cover many times.

And there are certain authors whom I admire. When I get the opportunity, I buy as many of their books as I can. The books I have read over and over have impacted my life. I take the authors as my mentors, even though they do not know me personally. When I read their books, I allow them to speak into my life. It does not mean that I necessarily agree with everything they say. Some of what they say is inapplicable and inappropriate to where I live. But I look for the timeless and universal principles they share. These are the nuggets I dig out of the books, which is really like picking their brains.

I hope that this book has *got through to you*. If it has, I will be satisfied that I have spoken into your life and your life has changed for the better.

Finally, here is something practical you can do: Get together with a few like-minded friends and discuss the ideas I have shared. Talk about becoming your own bosses. Talk about saving, business, and investing. Discuss and brainstorm on business ideas. Develop your plans together. I can guarantee you that such discussions will not only be intellectually stimulating and fruitful but life-changing as well.

www.ingramcontent.com/pod-product-compliance
Lightning Source LLC
Chambersburg PA
CBHW021408210526
45463CB00001B/276